VON MAUR®

HOW AN AMERICAN DEPARTMENT STORE
DARED TO DO THINGS DIFFERENTLY

MELINDA PRADARELLI

ISBN: 978-1-5323-2531-1

Library of Congress Control Number: 2016919562

Published by
VON MAUR®
6565 Brady Street
Davenport, Iowa 52806

www.vonmaur.com

©2017
Printed in USA

Book Design: Creative Mellen
Author: Melinda Pradarelli
Printer: Cedar Graphics
Photographer: Bill Adams

FOREWORD

When we first set out to preserve the history of our family business, our intention was to create something for our eyes only—a keepsake of sorts. But the more we learned, the more our friends and family urged us to share our company's story.

We are a fourth-generation, family-owned-and-operated department store company that has been fortunate enough to not only survive but to slowly expand in a rapidly changing retail environment. It all started with our family patriarch Charles Jacob von Maur and his business partners, Rowland H. Harned and Edward C. Pursel. They opened their first shop in 1887 in downtown Davenport, Iowa. Just before the Great Depression, they merged with Petersen's department store (circa 1872) to create a combined history of more than 140 years.

When you stop and think about the fact that we've been in the retail business since before Alexander Graham Bell invented the telephone, that 28 presidents have come and gone, that there have been two world wars, and Neil Armstrong walked on the moon, well, you begin to understand just how long we've been at this.

Over the years, we have seen recessions, buyouts, scale backs, and bankruptcies force many independent stores to close their doors. Through it all, generation after generation of

"Our department stores would never have survived without all of the loyal customers who stood by our side—many of them for decades. We want to thank each and every one of you for your years of patronage. We are grateful."

family members and associates have stood by our side and shared our vision for providing a high level of customer service and the latest fashions. Our founder's great grandson, Jim von Maur, now runs the business and represents the fourth generation of family leadership. During his tenure, he has continued our legacy of offering distinctive department store services (free gift wrap and shipping, no-interest credit cards, pianists in every store, and more) while moving us forward into new parts of the country and into new frontiers, such as our online business.

We hope this book offers an inside look at one of America's last independent department stores. It's a history filled with equal parts good luck and hard lessons. We dedicate this book to our wives, Nancy and Sue, and to all of the associates, customers, and family members who have taken this journey with us.

Chuck von Maur

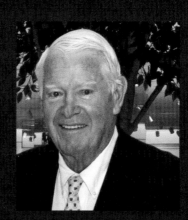
Dick von Maur

VON MAUR FAMILY TREE (Beginning with Company Founder C.J. von Maur)

CABLE G. VON MAUR

b. 12/29/1890 - d. 7/10/1965

Married Janette Lane
on 7/16/1913

JOSEPH L. VON MAUR

b. 12/7/1914 - d. 7/9/1992

Married Marjorie Ann Vernon
on 5/10/1941

MARY J. VON MAUR

b. 10//11/1917 - d. 12/6/1985

Married Fred Railsback
on 5/11/1943

JAMES W. VON MAUR

b. 1/5/1893 - d. 1/27/1965

Married Adelaide Carson
on 6/2/1920

MARY ADELAIDE VON MAUR

b. 5/16/1922

Married Edward W. Priester
on 2/23/1954

CHARLES JACOB (C.J.) VON MAUR

b. 2/15/1863 - d. 1/24/1926

Married Mary Ellen Cable
on 8/21/1889

RICHARD B. VON MAUR, SR.

b. 9/28/1896 - d. 12/14/1985

Married Elsie Wood
on 4/19/1927

GERTRUDE E. CRAMPTON

b. 6/13/1927 - d. 4/17/2011

Married Jerome S. Foy
on 11/29/1980

KATHERINE C. CRAMPTON

b. 2/16/1929

Married David Wolny
on 7/10/54

GEORGE W. CRAMPTON

b. 8/25/1930

Married Barbara Johnston
on 6/6/53

JOSEPHINE VON MAUR

b. 5/14/1902 - d. 2/24/1988

Married Albert Crampton
on 8/19/1926

CHARLES A. CRAMPTON

b. 11/30/1936

Company Founder Charles Jacob "C.J." von Maur started
Boston Store in 1887 with partners Rowland Harned and Edward
Pursel. C.J. had a vision for retail that became a foundation of
success for generations of von Maur family members.

ALICE B. VON MAUR

b. 2/7/1928

Married Don McDonald

on 9/19/1953

Married William Lewis
on 2/10/1988

Married Karen Jones
on 9/21/1990

HOLLY A. MCDONALD

b. 12/29/1955

Married John Senour
on 11/4/1978

BROOKE V.M. MCDONALD

b. 3/7/1960

Married Marc Mandhuit
on 8/9/1983

CHARLES R. VON MAUR

b. 4/8/1930

Married Nancy Frank
on 10/26/1957

HEATHER J. VON MAUR

b. 3/28/1964

Married Peter Tinsman
on 7/27/1988

ALLISON W. VON MAUR

b. 5/3/67
Married Mark Newcomb
on 6/6/2008

RICHARD B. VON MAUR III

b. 1/23/1967

Married Doreen McCorkle
on 5/31/2002

RICHARD B. VON MAUR, JR.

b. 5/26/1932

Married Susan Arp
on 6/14/1958

ROBIN B. VON MAUR

b. 6/14/1959

Married Lee Staak
on 2/4/1984

SUSAN A. VON MAUR

b. 1/25/1961
Married Holly Grimm, Jr.

on 4/16/1988

JAMES D. VON MAUR

b. 8/31/1969

Married Melissa Louise Berg
on 1/18/2000

4

TABLE OF CONTENTS

Harned Pursel & Von Maur
Boston Store opened in 1887.

J.H.C. Petersen & Sons store at the turn of the century.

Harned & Von Maur built
a new, three-story store in
Davenport, Iowa, in 1898.

(Photo courtesy of Davenport
Public Library)

chapter 1

"WHAT'S VON MAUR?"

"Von Maur? Really? It's a department store?"…"Where are they from?"… "How old are they?" "Did you say 1872?"…These are just some of the phrases countless people have murmured after hearing Von Maur is coming to a city near them and that the company has been in business for more than 140 years. Many have no idea Von Maur started as a dry goods store in Davenport, Iowa, in the late 1800s and has slowly, but surely, expanded to Chicago, Atlanta, Louisville, Birmingham, Rochester (New York), and beyond.

"I can't tell you how many times we've heard those questions from customers and city council members when we are looking at new markets," chuckles President James von Maur. Fortunately, that's just the way he and

his management team like it. The question gives "Jim," as he likes to be called, a nice big opening to explain that Von Maur is one of the last independent, family-owned-and-operated department stores in America. Some might wonder why Von Maur isn't flooding the markets with advertising to promote its name like other department store chains. But spend a few minutes at Von Maur headquarters and it quickly becomes apparent that understated elegance, both in the family's stores and in the way they conduct business, is a key component of the company culture.

One has to go back more than a century to understand how Von Maur grew from a small dry goods establishment to a popular downtown department store to a successful

C.J. von Maur and his business partners opened their first store in 1887 in downtown Davenport, Iowa. Just before the Great Depression, the company would merge with Petersen's department store (est. 1872) to create a combined history of more than 140 years.

This stained glass window from the 1893 Chicago's World Fair remains a central feature of the Von Maur headquarters in Davenport, Iowa.

national retail chain. For some, it's hard to even envision what department stores or their predecessors, the dry goods shops, looked like in the 1800s. But those who visit Von Maur headquarters on the outskirts of Davenport can catch a glimpse of the past. A beautiful stained glass window greets anyone who enters the doors. Measuring roughly 8 by 15 feet, the window features artwork and symbols representing the exchange of goods and services, including the staff of Mercury, the god of commerce and travel. It was originally created for and displayed in the palatial Manufactures and Liberal Arts Building at the Chicago World's Fair in 1893. The fair, which celebrated the 400th anniversary of Christopher Columbus' arrival in the New World, attracted more than 26 million visitors to Chicago.

One of those visitors was J.H.C. Petersen, who had traveled 180 miles from Davenport, where he ran a successful dry goods store. He knew the von Maurs; they ran a separate, competing retail store and were his rivals. What no one knew at the time was how closely intertwined the two families' destinies would become.

For decades, Petersen made the stained glass window the centerpiece of his downtown store, where it remained even after the 1928 merger of the Petersen and Harned & Von Maur stores. In 1990, when Von Maur opened its new corporate headquarters, the stained glass window, with its symbol of American entrepreneurism and invention, again was given a place of prominence. For more than 100 years, the window has been a proud reminder of the role the family and their department stores have played in the history of American retail and commerce. Few retailers today can claim to have roots in the mid-19th century; even fewer have managed to maintain family ownership.

Quality Goods at Honest Prices

The origin of the Von Maur department stores actually begins with Petersen some 30 years before the Chicago World's Fair. He started his career as a successful match manufacturer in northern Germany and shipped his products all over Europe. Petersen showed an early mastery of marketing by coloring his match heads with the national colors of the countries to which he exported them. Despite his savvy, he couldn't keep the business going when the value of Germany's currency plummeted after a failed revolt in the country. In 1860, with $3,000 in cash, Petersen and his family followed in the footsteps of hundreds of other German immigrants and traveled more than 4,500 miles to Iowa. His family landed in Maysville, Iowa, 11 miles northwest of Davenport.

J.H.C. Petersen established "Petersen's" as the place to shop in Davenport, Iowa, well before Boston Store opened its doors.

Petersen was industrious and had a strong work ethic, but he wasn't prepared for the American frontier. After three years, realizing he could not make it as a farmer, he moved his family to Davenport, already a booming river town perched along the Mississippi River. The city was home to about 20,000 people, and businesses as varied as ferryboat companies and flour mills were thriving. One newspaper described it as a hustle-and-bustle town, glowing with gas lamps and echoing with steam whistles. The city was experiencing a commercial boom that began six years earlier when it became home to the first railroad bridge across the Mississippi River. The railroad, as well as the growing number of steamboats loaded with people and goods, was changing the economy and future of this Iowa town. The period was marked by significant events in the life of the country as well. President Abraham Lincoln would sign the Emancipation Proclamation, the Pony Express would make its debut, and the Civil War would continue to tear the country apart.

Petersen briefly resurrected his small match company, but the business didn't fare well. Two larger companies dominated the market and within a decade would consolidate to become the Diamond Match Company. Petersen simply could not compete. Ever the entrepreneur, he quit the match business and tried his hand at merchandising. He formed a brief partnership with Henry Abel selling goods at auction, but his real dream was to launch a store with his sons, Max, Henry, and William. In 1872, he opened J.H.C. Petersen

Above: In the late 1800s, Davenport was a booming river town perched along the Mississippi River.

(Photo courtesy of Davenport Public Library)

& Sons Co. The store, which became known as Petersen's, occupied a small, 20- by 50-foot space in downtown Davenport with a working capital of just $1,400. To stock the store, Petersen and his sons attended auctions in Chicago and hauled goods, such as hats, caps, and notions, back to Davenport. Since retailers had to pay cash at auctions and had limited capital, their loads were small. That meant merchandise didn't last long on Petersen's shelves, and each week a member of the firm had to make the laborious trip back to Chicago to attend another auction.

In the late 1800s and early 1900s, dry goods stores were not the sprawling, air-conditioned arenas of retail we know today. They were small and dimly lit, relying on candles and gas lamps or, in rare cases, the modern marvel of electric arc lights. In order to see the true color or shape of a piece of merchandise, customers often had to walk it over to one of the store's windows and inspect it in natural light. Despite these shortcomings, stores offered such a rich variety of goods that customers visited as much to look and socialize as to buy. Petersen's sold bolts of fabric customers used to sew their own clothes, drapes, and bedding. There were buttons, bows, bindings, silk, lace, ribbons, china, and glassware. There were some, but not many, ready-made items such as gloves, shawls, and blankets. Over time, many stores added toys, ceramic dishes, and books, but it wasn't until much later that they sold items such as suits and dresses. Petersen's store motto was "Quality Goods at Honest Prices."

Mail Order Catalogs and Five-and-Dimes

The same year Petersen started his dry goods store, Aaron Montgomery Ward established the first mail-order catalog business. Within six years, another famous merchant, Frank W. Woolworth, introduced the new concept of discount stores that featured a selection of merchandise priced at five and ten cents. This set the stage for the development of national retail chains. Already a rivalry was emerging between small, independent stores like Petersen's and fast-growing national chains like Woolworth that would shape the landscape of American retail throughout the next century.

(Photo courtesy of Davenport Public Library)

The family couldn't afford to hire book-keepers, cashiers, clerks, bundle-wrappers, or even a porter and, consequently, had to do all of the work themselves. There was no delivery system, not even by horse. It was not uncommon to see one or all three of the Petersen boys trudging along the streets with large bundles under their arms. They often made deliveries after nightfall since their presence was required behind the counter during the day. Some nights the boys made up their beds under the store counters so they would be available in case a customer stopped by. Their efforts and experience paid off. Over the next 12 years, Petersen's expanded and began operating branch stores in the nearby towns of Geneseo, Illinois, and Clinton, Iowa. By 1887, Petersen's had 125 employees and sales that claimed to be "without doubt the largest of any house of the kind in the state."

Above: Petersen's 1894 newsletter and early 1900s advertisement.

An inside look at Petersen's turn-of-the-century display area.

chapter 2

VON MAUR AND PARTNERS LAUNCH BOSTON STORE

(1888-1926)

J.H.C. Petersen & Sons Co. was about to face a worthy competitor in Davenport. In 1887, three businessmen announced plans to launch a new dry goods store just a block away from the established retailer. One of those men was 24-year-old Charles Jacob "C.J." von Maur, who was born in 1863 in Saugerties, New York. Reared to be hardworking, thrifty, and self-reliant, C.J. dabbled in dry goods sales while he was still in high school and, at 17, became a store manager at a local store. Bright and gifted with a head for numbers, he could add and multiply complicated sums in seconds. Over the next five years, he studied at a Scranton, Pennsylvania, business college, took his first full-time job at a small store in Pittston, Pennsylvania, and at just 22, launched a new business with a young

man in nearby Plymouth. That venture ended abruptly when his partner died of typhoid fever.

The tragedy prompted C.J. to move across the state to Wilkes-Barre, Pennsylvania, to work at the thriving Fowler, Dick and Walker, a store specializing in fine groceries, quality sundries, and clothing. Fowler, as the store was often known, had opened in 1879, and quickly became the largest dry goods store in Wilkes-Barre. This was where C.J. met future business partners Rowland H. Harned and Edward C. Pursel. Harned, known for his steady judgment, was born in Shickshinny, Pennsylvania, where his father worked in real estate. After a course of study at the Wyoming Seminary and graduating from Wyoming Commercial College, Harned became a

Over the years, the von Maurs have collected everything from antique cash registers and carousel horses to sleighs and brass fire extinguishers. Many of these items, which they still display at their headquarters today, were featured in their downtown Davenport store and in their first mall stores.

15

Employees gather outside the Harned & Von Maur
Boston Store in the late 1800s.

It was just a year after the Harned Pursel & Von Maur Boston Store opened that the term "department store" entered the American lexicon. It appeared in a July 1888 *New York Times* article to describe a new store opening in Los Angeles.

salesman and later assistant manager at Fowler, where he worked for five years. Little is known of Pursel beyond the fact that he hailed from Pennsylvania, most likely Doylestown, and that his young partners liked and trusted him. All three were ambitious and in April 1887, the trio moved to Davenport.

Boston Store

With their combined assets, Harned, Pursel, and von Maur opened Boston Store in 1887. The store, which was just a little smaller than an average-sized tennis court, was at the corner of Second and Brady streets. Second Street had become the place to shop in the river town, and one main draw was the well-established Petersen's store. It's probably safe to assume that the three young entrepreneurs were a little daunted by the prospect of competing against the thriving retailer. Petersen's shelves were filled with the latest fashions and goods. By comparison, Boston Store had a stock valued at less than $15,000 on opening day. The wares included draperies, rugs, cut glass, crockery, lamps, and glassware. As it turns out, there was plenty of business for both stores. "It was a pretty apt illustration," Harned was quoted as saying, "of the old adage about great oaks and little acorns, for we found it necessary to make additions every six months for the first two years. Within three years, our store had grown to eight times its original size."

C.J. von Maur was 24 years old when he moved from Pennsylvania to Iowa to help found Boston Store.

Rowland Harned, born in Shickshinny, Pennsylvania, came from a family of retailers. His extended family helped run Zollinger-Harned department store in Allentown, Pennsylvania, for decades before it closed in 1978.

Edward Pursel was born near Doylestown, Pennsylvania, and died just two years after Boston Store opened. (Image not available)

In just three years, the Harned Pursel & Von Maur Boston Store had grown to eight times its original size.

Many have wondered why Harned, Pursel, and von Maur named their first shop Boston Store. Some later assumed it was part of The Boston Store that as of 2015 was owned by the Bon-Ton Stores, Inc. group. Few knew that "Boston Store" was actually a generic term used to refer to a store that sold fine goods or imported fabrics. Fowler, Dick and Walker had included the phrase "Boston Store" at the end of its name in much the way the term "department store" would later be used. Harned, Pursel, and von Maur didn't want to use their surnames for their new store, so they simply called it Boston Store. The store was just beginning to flourish when, in January 1889, tragedy struck. Pursel cut himself while using a knife to open a shipping crate and bled to death. He was 26 years old. Mourning the loss of their good friend, Harned and von Maur continued to manage the store. Over the next four years, Boston Store would take root in Davenport and double in size.

New Buildings. Big Changes.

Boston Store's growing presence would certainly have been on the minds of Petersen and his sons as they traveled back to Davenport from the Chicago World's Fair in 1893. Petersen had retired from the family business, but wanted to help put the finishing touches on the family's new four-story store. He left the World's Fair inspired by the buildings American architect Daniel Burnham had created. Back in Davenport, fueled by the innovations and opulence they had seen at the fair, Petersen and his sons spared no expense in completing the family's new store. Soon, customers in carriages could pull up to the store's stone archway entrance that rose two stories above the sidewalk. Inside, there was an ornamental, pressed-tin ceiling, Corinthian columns, carved wood counters, a grand staircase, and the stained glass window purchased at the fair. Eventually a tearoom was added, done in Flemish oak and featuring a soda fountain made of marble and bronze. Customers could buy "for one price and at the lowest" everything from velvet piping to sheet music published by Petersen's. Slogans about service and value were printed on the wrapping paper used to bundle customers' purchases. Associates rang up merchandise on ornate bronze cash registers, which remain part of the Von Maur corporate office memorabilia.

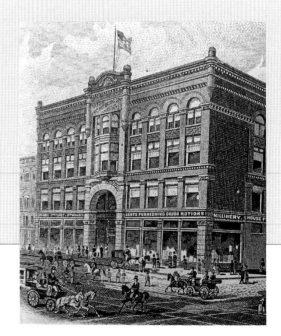

Exterior rendering of J.H.C. Petersen's circa 1800s.

Major department stores competed for business in downtown Davenport in the late 1800s.

Above: The main floor of J.H.C Petersen & Sons on opening day.

In 1898, partners Harned and von Maur
opened a new, three-story store in downtown
Davenport bearing their names.

Harned, Bergner & Von Maur

Not to be outdone, Harned and von Maur began looking for ways to expand. In 1894, they partnered with another, now prominent, retailer by the name of Peter A. Bergner who founded Bergner department stores in Peoria, Illinois, five years earlier. The three men renamed the existing Peoria store Harned, Bergner and Von Maur. The wholesale and retail business sold dry goods, including cloaks and millinery, and operated for about 12 years, until 1906. Not much is known about the partnership, but Harned and von Maur must have spent some time at the Peoria store, because it was reported the two men narrowly escaped a tornado that nearly blasted the tin roof off the store, causing a fire to break out. The local newspaper went on to report that Harned and von Maur tried to "roll the roof back" to stop the fire from spreading.

Two years after beginning this new partnership, Harned and von Maur still had greater aspirations. They bought a lot at the corner of Second and Harrison streets in Davenport and spent more than a year guiding construction of a new, three-story building. The store opened on Oct. 20, 1898, under the name Harned & Von Maur. Like most stores in that day, it was closed on Sundays in honor of the so-called "Sabbath Law" passed in 1857. This law forbade, among

other things, dancing, shooting, hunting, fishing, buying, selling, or doing anything but essential work on Sunday. The penalty was a fine of between $1 and $5 until 1870, when the House of Representatives passed a bill increasing the penalty to between $5 and $100. For decades, C.J. was adamant there would be no sales on Sundays. He even pulled the curtains closed on the store so that people passing by couldn't window shop. The only time his grandsons remember him opening the store on a Sunday was to find a shirt for a man who needed to attend a funeral. He gave the man the shirt and wouldn't accept money for it because he believed he couldn't, and shouldn't, sell anything on Sunday.

In 1889, Peter Bergner founded Bergner's department store in downtown Peoria, Illinois. In 1991, P.A. Bergner & Co. filed for Chapter 11 bankruptcy. Upon emerging from bankruptcy in 1993, it began operating under Carson Pirie Scott & Co.

(Photo courtesy of *Peoria Journal Star*)

The Harned & Von Maur Boston Store sat at the heart
of a bustling downtown Davenport in the late 1800s.

(Photo courtesy Putnam Museum of History and
Natural Science)

R.H. Harned, A Poem

The shoppers' money dribbles out

While Harned's cash comes pouring in;

He doesn't mind the weather bleak,

The surging crowds, the Yuletide din.

Other folks may grouch and gloom

With empty purses and hacking cough;

At Christmas time he always wears

This happy smile that won't come off.

As C.J. was running the thriving store, he was becoming known as a firm but fair retailer. He was slowly developing the values that would stay with the next three generations of von Maurs. "Treat every customer like family; commit to quality and service; Rule No. 1 is the customer is always right; and Rule No. 2 is if you think the customer is wrong, refer back to Rule No. 1."

Petersen Passes

In 1905, J.H.C. Petersen died at the age of 88, and his sons took over the business. Over the next few years, Petersen's and Harned & Von Maur would continue to grow their businesses through President Theodore Roosevelt's administration, the advent of the skyscraper, and the introduction of the celebrated Model T Ford. Harned & Von Maur was beginning to introduce the special touches that later became a hallmark. Women could have their hair dressed, free of charge, at the beauty parlor, and men could have their shoes shined. The store was doing well. A 1910 ad states, "In volume of business, last week was one of the greatest in the history of this establishment. More people visited this store last Saturday than any other single day before. Our Fourth Semi-Annual, 20 Percent Cash Discount Sale closed with new records, set high above others…"

Above: This cartoon, which appeared in the local newspaper, depicts Harned seated atop the six-story Harned & Von Maur store building holding up a flag labeled, "A Corner for the People." The poem and cartoon about the young Rowland Harned was published in "A Portfolio of Cartoons" by the *Davenport Times* 1912-1913. Verses by Irving C. Norwood.

(Photo courtesy of Putnam Museum of History and Natural Science)

Harned & Von Maur again took a step forward in 1911 when it completed a three-story addition to its store. The store now featured mahogany and mission décor, as well as three electric elevators, sprinklers for fire protection, mail order for out-of-town shoppers, and cash tubes. For many department stores, these tubes became indispensable for moving cash, coins, messages, and even small items of merchandise to precise locations. A good-sized store often had between 16 to 18 miles of tubing. The tubes were a fun novelty, but they also served another purpose. Many store owners didn't think associates were capable of handling cash or making change, so they required them to put cash in the tube at the checkout and send it to a central cashier area. So, while the tubes may have been entertaining to some, the truth was that neither customers nor associates enjoyed how long it took to complete a purchase. Eventually, cash registers came onto the scene and displaced the cash tubes.

The Lighter Side of Retail

Harned and von Maur weren't above using a little subterfuge to improve their odds against their rivals. C.J. was known to put empty boxes on the shelves so that Petersen's would think Harned and Von Maur had a bigger inventory than it did.

C.J. also spent a good deal of time keeping order at the store. His brother, Henry, was known for using his fists to settle things when they didn't go his way. More often than not this happened when C.J. was away on a buying trip, and Henry was left in charge. Traditionally, the stock boys would pick up a broom and clean the store before the customers first arrived. But they wouldn't sweep the floor for Henry. So Henry was known to give them a "poke in the nose" to get them started in the right direction.

Pictured above are the cash tubes Harned & Von Maur used to transport money from the shop floor to the cashier.

Above left to right: R.H. Harned, C.J. von Maur, and Henry W. von Maur.

Davenport's Foremost Department Store

*Easily Reached From All
Street Cars and Depots.*

Harned & Von Maur

2nd and Harrison Streets

52 Stores in One

Petersen's and Harned & Von Maur were running neck-and-neck, trying to outdo one another with merchandise and advertising. In 1912, Petersen's advertised, "Never before in the history of our business have we had such a collection of knobby, snappy models as this coming season," while Harned & Von Maur called attention to "52 stores in one." As World War I approached, the good times were about to come to an end, particularly for the Petersens. Max Petersen died in 1914, followed a year later by the death of his brother, Henry. William, 64, the youngest of the three brothers, was left to carry on alone. In 1916, at the height of the war, he sold the family business to Harned & Von Maur. In a handshake deal (no paperwork was ever found), Harned & Von Maur purchased the Petersen stock for $609,000, marking the largest mercantile transaction in the history of Davenport. *The Davenport Democrat and Leader* reported, "The combined buying power coupled with the current wholesale system will be of tremendous benefit and naturally place both stores in a position to buy at lower prices than concerns lacking such advantages."

One Owner. Two Businesses.

Davenport's two oldest department stores now had one owner. C.J. became president of both firms; Harned, vice president; and Cable, C.J.'s son, secretary. For shoppers, little changed. Each store continued to carry its original name and operate independently for the next 12 years. The stores were selling a lot of overcoats, suits, dresses, and brassieres, as well as the latest rage, the phonograph. Both also had wholesale businesses, which meant salesmen for the two stores traveled throughout Iowa and into Illinois and Nebraska, selling company linens and other products. Cars were scarce so most of the wholesale business involved traveling to small, rural communities by horse and buggy. Back in Davenport, Cable began to play a more pivotal role in the business, and one of his biggest jobs was hiring personnel. In 1918, he hired Madeline "Maddy" Roenfeldt when she was just 15. Maddy, who worked for the company for decades in nearly every department, said the most interesting position she held was as store interpreter for the large number of shoppers who immigrated to Davenport from Germany. The von Maurs had a translator on staff for years to help provide better service to German-speaking customers.

In 1922, the Mississippi River once again overflowed its banks, flooding the downtown and Harned & Von Maur. The department store was among the tallest buildings in the city, so many people used the store's upper floors to seek safe haven from the rising water below. The floods were a setback but did not stop two big celebrations that year: Harned & Von Maur had been open for 35 years, and Petersen's hit 50. For the first time, customers could buy fine china on a club plan, allowing them to pay off the merchandise in small weekly payments. Other sale items included: Smartest Silk Frocks, $17.50 each; Sexton Athletic Union Suits, 95 cents; Mercerized Pongee Men's Shirts, $2.15; and Jersey bathing suits for women, $5. There were also specials for owners of small cars, including spark plugs, running-board luggage carriers, Sun Ray lenses, Ford Touring sedan seat covers, Little Giant tire pumps, as well as car jacks and speedometers. On June 30, 1922, an ad showcased everything from advice on dressing properly for Fourth of July to the latest enameled ware for making preserves.

By 1923, another formidable competitor, the M.L. Parker Company, moved into a seven-story department store just a block away from Petersen's. Parker's, as it was known,

William D. Petersen, son of J.H.C. Petersen, was well-respected in Davenport and was seldom seen without a black cigar clamped between his teeth.

(Photo courtesy of the *Father of the Davenport Levee* by Hugh Harrison)

Harned & Von Maur's 75th Diamond Jubilee window depicts wares from 1872 to 1910.

featured extensive lines of merchandise and introduced popular new "three-person" elevators. On sale days, shoppers could take nonstop elevator rides to a special sales area on the fifth floor. Retail competition was heating up in Davenport, and C.J. and Harned were beginning to entrust more of the business to the von Maur sons, Cable, James, and Richard, who were in their 30s and involved in all aspects of the business.

In Memoriam

In spring of 1925, having left detailed plans for how the stores should operate in his absence, C.J., his wife, and their daughter, Josephine, left on a three-month trip to Egypt. C.J. contracted malaria on the trip, an illness he battled for months before his physician sent him to Hot Springs, Arkansas, for treatment. Five weeks later, in January 1926, C.J. died at the Arlington Hotel in Hot Springs at the age of 63. C.J. would be remembered as someone who had made a significant impact not only in the world of retail, but also on his family and the community.

chapter 3

MERGERS, ACQUISITIONS, AND A SELL-OFF THAT SAVES THE BUSINESS

(1927-1949)

The Petersen and Harned & Von Maur stores closed for a day to honor founder C.J.'s death. When they reopened, the sons realized they faced an interesting challenge that had nothing to do with merchandise. How, associates were heard to ask, should they refer to their three new bosses—who were all known as "Mr. von Maur?" The solution? Call them Mr. Cable, Mr. Jim and Mr. Dick[1]. The tradition of using "Mr." followed by one of the von Maur's first names continues to this day.

The brothers also started another family tradition that called for the oldest son to be named president of the company. In this case, that was Cable, who was born in Davenport in 1890 and went on to join the family business after attending Culver Military School and earning his law degree from State University of Iowa (now the University of Iowa). All of the von Maur brothers were fairly reserved but, in time, Cable emerged as the company spokesperson and became deeply involved in community affairs. At the store, he was in charge of shoes and men's wear and oversaw the Budget and Basement stores. James W. (Jim), born in 1893, attended Iowa State College, and was a pilot during World War I. He preferred to work behind the scenes and focused his talents on store operations and home furnishings. Dick Sr. was born in 1896 and attended Iowa State College and Wharton School of Finance and Commerce in Philadelphia. Over the years, he would help grow the business dramatically, becoming involved in everything from the

[1]*Mr. Dick is referred to as Dick Sr. in future references. His son is referred to as Dick.*

To Prepare!

--for the greatest selling
event in the Tri-Cities' history

CLOSED

The Harned & Von Maur Store
closed permanently at
5:30 o'clock today

GETTING READY

Petersen's Store--now
Petersen-Harned-Von Maur

will reopen next
Tuesday, June 12
at 8:30, for the great

Merger Sale

14 Pages in the Tri-City papers
Monday give the details

Petersen~Harned~Von Maur

A few months after the merger,
merchandise from both
stores had been moved to the
existing Petersen building at
Second and Main Street.

Cable von Maur

President

The oldest brother, Cable von Maur, became president and was married to Janette Lane. They had two children, Joseph (Joe) and Mary. Joe worked in men's merchandising at Petersen's for 25 years.

way merchandise was displayed to internal operations. Through it all, he was methodical about his interest and understanding of retail. He eventually took over feminine apparel.

Petersen Harned Von Maur

In 1928, two years after C.J.'s death, Petersen's and Harned & Von Maur merged and began to operate under a new name: Petersen Harned Von Maur. The von Maurs and Harned adopted the lengthy name because they didn't want to alienate customers loyal to either store. And frankly, this was just one more store name in a long line of them. Since 1887, the company had been known by a handful of names, both formally and informally, including Harned, Pursel & Von Maur; Boston Store; Harned, Bergner & Von Maur; Harned & Von Maur; Harned & Von Maur/J.H.C. Petersen & Sons (two stores); and now Petersen Harned Von Maur. The reality was that within days of changing the name to Petersen Harned Von Maur, loyal customers took it upon themselves to come up with a shorter, easier title, and adopted the name Petersen's, or simply Pete's, as the store was referred to for decades to come.

The May 7, 1928, store merger occurred just six months before Iowan Herbert Hoover was elected president. *A Davenport Democrat and Leader* headline read, "The combined store carries stock in excess of $1 million." By

James von Maur, Sr.

Richard von Maur, Sr.

An Adventurous Spirit

James W. (Jim), born in 1893, attended Iowa State College and was a pilot during World War I. He preferred to work behind the scenes and focused his talents on store operations and home furnishings. Although he was a quiet man, Jim was known for his adventurous spirit. He enjoyed recreational flying, as well as skiing and riding motorcycles. In 1920, he married Adelaide Carson and they had a daughter, Mary Adelaide.

A True Merchant

Richard (Dick) Sr., who served in World War I, was considered the true merchant of the family and a student of retail. Unfortunately, family obligations kept him from completing his college degree at Wharton School of Finance and Commerce in Philadelphia. While at Wharton, his father asked him to return home briefly to attend his brother's wedding. The event conflicted with a required Wharton test he would not be able to retake. Hearing this, C.J. reminded his son that family came first. Dick Sr. attended the wedding and did not return to Wharton. In 1927, he married Elsie Wood, and they had three children, Alice, Chuck, and Dick.

By the time Dick Sr. began working at Harned & Von Maur, his brothers were already deeply entrenched in store operations. So it's no surprise they played a trick on him his first day. They told him to unroll a new cheesecloth shipment to ensure it measured 100 yards. He worked from 7:30 a.m. to 12:30 p.m., creating a mountain of slippery cheesecloth that measured 103 yards. He proudly reported his findings to his brothers who laughed and told him to spend the rest of the day rolling the material back up.

comparison, Harned, von Maur, and Pursel had opened Boston Store 40 years earlier with $15,000 in stock. Combining Davenport's two largest stores elevated the company to a new level in Iowa, comparable to department stores such as Younker Brothers and Harris-Emery in Des Moines, Davidson's in Sioux City, and Killian's in Cedar Rapids.

On June 12, 1928, a month after the merger was announced, Petersen Harned Von Maur (henceforth referred to as Petersen's) opened its new, consolidated store. Merchandise from both stores had been moved to the existing Petersen building at Second and Main streets. Now longtime customers of both stores could find everything they needed in one location. The owners promoted the opening with a 14-page advertising insert in the Tri-City papers. The featured item was a refrigerator with the capacity to hold 50 lbs. of ice on sale for $29.75. The von Maurs and Harned knew that customers would flock to their new store to see the ice-capacity refrigerator, which was just beginning to make its way into the average home. While customers expected to find the latest fashions and furnishings at the store, they may have been surprised at the level of service. The new store doubled its staff to 450 employees.

This was an exciting year to be an American. In the months surrounding the opening

Harned & Von Maur's original 1913 downstairs store was advertised as the Bargain Basement.

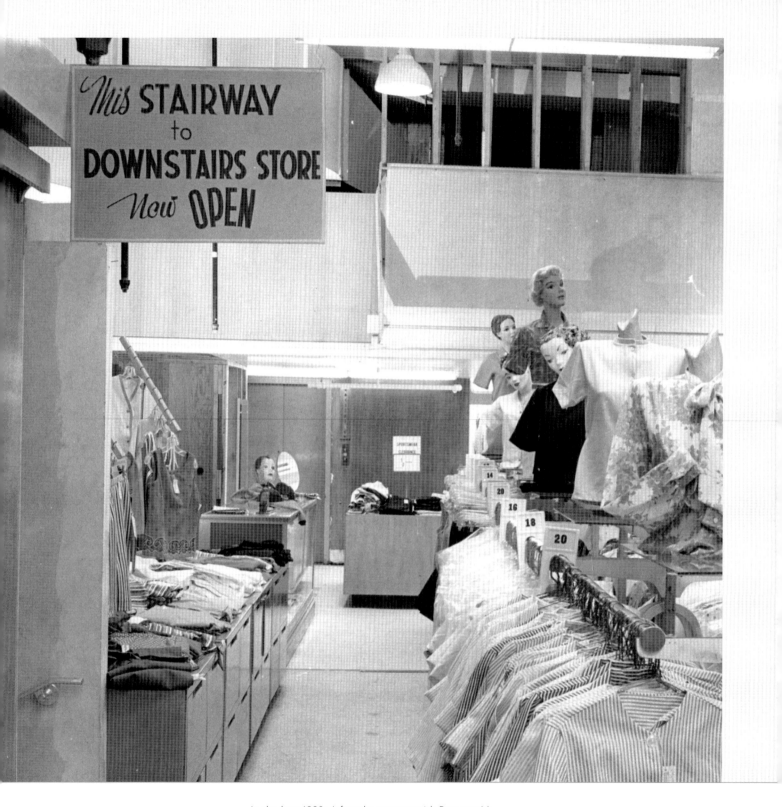

In the late 1920s (after the merger with Petersen's)
the lower level was reconfigured to create a tearoom,
a shoe repair shop, and the new Downstairs Store.

The New *Majestic*

Only Majestic could offer this great new improvement—incorporated in sensationally beautiful new cabinet designs—at still lower prices—because only Majestic has the tremendous facilities, the stupendous buying power necessary to offer quality radio sets at the lowest prices for quality merchandise that the world has ever known! This Great New Speaker—These Great New Prosperity Models—at Amazingly Lower Prices—That Only Majestic Could Offer!

MODEL 91
(ILLUSTRATED ABOVE)

of the new store, Walt Disney introduced Mickey Mouse to the public, Amelia Earhart became the first woman to fly across the Atlantic, and George Eastman exhibited the first color motion pictures in the United States. Back in Davenport, the von Maur sons were trying to find new and innovative ways to serve long-standing customers. Some of the innovations were reflected in the store's floor plan. The lower level was reconfigured to create a tearoom, a shoe repair shop, and the new Downstairs Store (a variation on the Bargain Basement that had occupied the previous Harned & Von Maur store since at least 1913.)

Upstairs, Petersen's featured a much broader line of goods, including one of America's newer innovations—the radio. Throughout the 1920s, families enjoyed listening to baseball games, church services, concerts, and their favorite weekly radio shows in the comfort of their living rooms. By 1928, *Billboard Magazine* had published its first charts and the radio was here to stay. Within a year, Petersen's had sold more Majestic Radios than any other store in Iowa. As the size of the store and the staff continued to grow, Cable, Jim, and Dick Sr. had to find better ways to stay connected to the staff. Dozens of department heads now oversaw everything from men's and women's apparel to home furnishings. Each night after the store closed, the brothers gathered at the landing of the store's grand staircase to thank all of the employees for their work. They also collected the day's receipts, which they manually tabulated each night, since there were no computers.

Purchasing Fisk and Loosley

Retail sales remained strong at Petersen's even as the nation's economy began to soften. Riding their recent merger success, the sons purchased a department store in 1929 in Moline, Illinois, called Fisk and Loosley. In its earlier days, the store had been an architectural jewel of the downtown, but over the years it had not been well maintained.

Dick Sr. was known for mentoring his children and those outside of the family. He helped guide many young store associates, among them William A. Andres, who worked in the company's Basement Store for about three years. Andres left Petersen's in 1958 and ultimately joined Dayton's department store. He rose to become the first CEO outside the Dayton family to head the Minneapolis-based retail firm. In 2000, Dayton–Hudson was renamed Target Corporation.

By 1929, when the von Maurs purchased the store, the building had been in disrepair for years. Still, the purchase appeared to be prudent. Moline was just 15 minutes from Davenport and seemed a natural place to expand the business. Customers in Moline already shopped at the von Maur's Davenport store, so the brothers expected an easy transition to the new store, which would retain the name Fisk and Loosley. They were taken aback at the welcome they received. From the minute they bought the store, city officials demanded the company make upgrades. The von Maurs had completed the purchase thinking the building was sound and ready to occupy. They were not prepared to spend a lot of money to revamp the building. After all, as the 1920s drew to a close, even before the stock market crash,

economists were already seeing problems for department store operations, because costs were rising. The period of intense department store growth ended right after World War I. As the author of *Service and Style* wrote, "The mid-1920s were good years, and there would be a few very profitable periods in the future but, for the most part, big stores would face daunting challenges as aggressive competitors rose up, costs increased, and suburban living, combined with downtown traffic congestion, took away customers."

As the von Maurs struggled to regain ground in Moline, the Great Depression hit the nation. More than 800 Iowa banks folded between 1929 and 1933. Unemployment on a national level was estimated at between 4 to 5 million. Almost overnight, store

Above: A trolley delivers customers to Fisk and Loosley. From 1929 to 1933, total retail sales in the United States declined by half, dropping from $48.5 to $24.5 billion. Although some department stores made a profit, the majority, like the Petersen's, experienced devastating losses.

(Photo courtesy of *Moline: City of Mills*, 1998 Arcadia Publishing)

By the Numbers

In the early days, Petersen's conducted an inventory accounting once a year, a process that took between two to four weeks. This was decades before computers, which meant inventory was a slow and painstaking process. Each shelf in each department contained a yellow piece of paper with handwritten information about what items should be on the shelf and when they were first placed there. When items sold, associates marked them off the yellow sheet. Once a year, all the yellow sheets were collected and taken upstairs to a large room where 12 to 14 women combed through them, using comptometers to account for what had been sold. If there was a discrepancy between the items on the shelf and the yellow sheet, store associates would scour their departments for the missing pieces. When asked how accurate this system was, the von Maur brothers said with a laugh, "It was accurate within tolerance."

sales dried up. Few people could afford to buy anything extra—let alone some of the higher-end merchandise the store carried. This was particularly true for wholesale business customers such as small merchants and rural customers. Many of these customers were farmers struggling to hold onto their land as the price of corn, beans, and hogs plummeted. Petersen's salesmen took orders for future deliveries, only to have them canceled by small merchants unable to pay.

The continuing controversy with the city also took a toll on sales in Moline. The von Maurs had to make a choice or risk losing everything. After securing a loan from a Boston bank through a family connection, they decided to shut down Fisk and Loosley. In 1932, as President Herbert Hoover tried desperately to stem the Great Depression by granting generous credit to industry and ordering a stern check on government spending, the von Maurs brought the entire stock of the Moline store to Davenport for a giant disposal sale.

Early Customer Connections

The family's store weathered this economic disaster in large part because of the customer relationships fostered by its employees. One of the early floorwalkers, Fred Bode, took his reputation to the grave. His obituary read, "It was said of him that he never forgot a face, and that he knew by name over half of the residents of Scott County." Another associate, Myrtle Johnson, knew by heart the hosiery size of nearly every customer who walked in the door. In May 1934, a year after Prohibition ended, the nation was hit with record cold snaps in the winter and searing heat in the summer, creating one of the most destructive droughts in the Midwest. But the weather could not dampen citizens' optimism that the country was beginning to recover from the Depression. Petersen's celebrated its 62nd Anniversary Sale. The first customers received birthday cakes, and dozens of extra employees were on hand to handle the large crowds. The day began when the store's display windows were unveiled to reveal a pictorial history of the Petersen and Harned & Von Maur stores, created by Davenport artist Lou Weisbrook.

The anniversary allowed the store to usher in a host of new services, including a dress pattern section, bakery department, linen department, beauty shop, improved apparel section, watch repair room, and an enhanced tearoom. Petersen's was gaining momentum—and customers—when, in 1937, Harned died. The following year the Harned family sold its interest in the business to the von Maurs. Since that day, the business has been a private, single-family-owned operation, though its stores would bear the name Petersen Harned Von Maur until 1989.

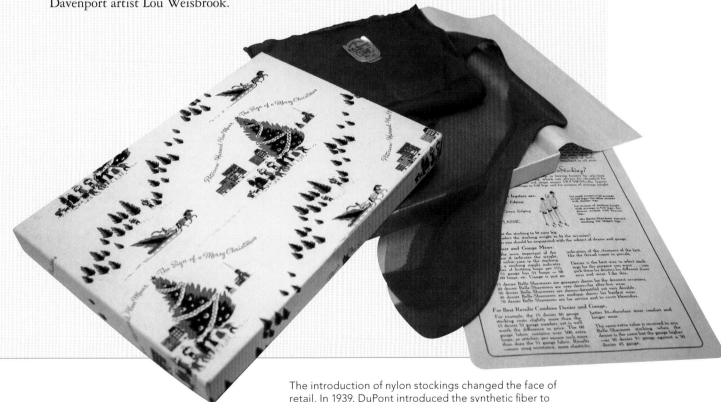

The introduction of nylon stockings changed the face of retail. In 1939, DuPont introduced the synthetic fiber to 3,000 women's club members at the New York World's Fair. Soon department stores, such as Petersen's, would have entire sections dedicated to hosiery sales. Above is an original package of Petersen's stockings, complete with gift box and care instructions.

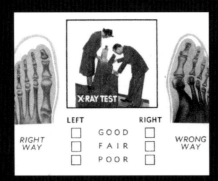

Shoe-fitting Fluoroscope

In the 1930s, '40s, and '50s, the shoe-fitting fluoroscope was a common fixture within Petersen's children's shoe department and in retailers nationwide. Now, customers could have their feet x-rayed for size. The typical machine had an opening near the bottom where customers could insert their feet. The viewing ports at the top allowed the child, the parent, and the salesperson to all see an image of the bones of the feet and the outline of the shoes. Chuck and Dick von Maur recall with a laugh that they spent hours using the machine to x-ray their feet. In the late 1940s and early 1950s, safety concerns compelled department stores to remove the technology.

The brothers were now at the helm of the business, and they celebrated the store's 10-year-old merger with full-page ads touting new products and services. The store featured everything from books to ready-to-wear to a tearoom touted as "the city's most distinctive luncheon spot."

World War II

In the spring of 1941, months before the Japanese bombed Pearl Harbor, Petersen's advertised, "This is our own, our native look," showing jacket dresses with shoulder pads and tweed or camel hair coats for $19.95. Soon the United States was drawn into World War II, which brought an official end to the depression years as the nation's industries geared up for full-scale wartime production. It wasn't easy running a department store during the war. In some cases, stores limited the number of items they could sell to a customer in a day. There were days when Petersen's customers could only buy one of the popular, but rationed, nylon stockings they desperately wanted. One associate recalls having to lock up the nylons each night in order to keep the merchandise safe.

On May 2, 1942, while the war raged on, the von Maurs faced another challenge. The store was set to celebrate its 70th anniversary, but the national rationing of everything from sugar and coffee to gasoline limited the variety of available merchandise. Still, the store moved forward with an anniversary sale ad in *The Davenport Daily Times* that stated, "A sale in the midst of a war. In many instances manufacturers who dealt with Petersen's for a quarter of a century or more have shown their recognition of the importance of the 70th anniversary sale by providing offerings that would seem impossible at the present time." The hardships of war meant shoppers—and retailers—had to be innovative when it came to finding items they were unwilling to do without. In 1944, a woman from Rock Island took the ferry, which cost 5 cents, across the Mississippi River to Petersen's to buy a wedding dress. The dress cost $25—a third of her monthly salary. She made a $3.75 down payment and for several weeks traveled by ferry, paying installments until the account was settled. The couple married the next day.

The Glove Department

In addition to the growing demand for nylon stockings, fashion swung nationwide during World War II toward bare midriffs, slim skirts, and large hats. Another "must-have" item continued to be women's gloves. Gloves were essential components of a lady's wardrobe, worn whenever she went out in public. But there was an art to fitting women with gloves. The gloves sold by the von Maurs were made from kidskin, a soft leather made from the skin of a young goat. Fresh out of the package, they were very tight. To ensure a good fit, it was imperative that the clerks spent time fitting women for their gloves— one finger at a time—using a glove stretcher. It was not uncommon to have more than a dozen shoppers lined up in the glove department awaiting their fitting.

The von Maur family was deeply involved in the community. For decades, they extended a discount to clergy and their families. A religious man, C.J. believed he and his family should do everything they could to support area pastors. During WWII, Harned & Von Maur became active in war bond sales. By July 1943, the store's 412 employees had helped to sell $116,163 in war stamps and bonds.

Postwar Excitement

Like the rest of the world in the mid-1940s, Davenport's citizens eagerly awaited news about the war. When Victory Day in Europe arrived in 1945, Dick Sr. and the store display director hurried downtown to create a victory window with the Statue of Liberty, doves, and all the trimmings. In that era, department stores were very much at the center of community events. Hundreds of people gathered outside the store windows to celebrate, and soon larger quantities of merchandise slowly began to return to the shelves. Two years later, the von Maurs prepared for the store's Diamond Jubilee Celebration. Looking back on 75 years of successful business, they attributed it all to "adhering to the ideals of the founders for truth, friendliness, fair play, and good values," calling attention to its "roots buried deep in the life of the community."

Petersen's celebrated 75 years with
a Diamond Jubilee event in 1947.

Customers flooded the store during
Petersen's 75-year celebration.

chapter 4

AT A CROSSROADS

(1950-1974)

By the 1950s, downtowns and department stores had become synonymous with one another. Downtowns were thriving centers of commerce that for decades had attracted people to shop at competing department stores that operated within blocks of one another. But that began to change as more people bought cars and the highway systems expanded. Shoppers could now get from one place to another faster, paving the way for a new American concept—suburbia.

The postwar buying spree was over. It was time to reevaluate the company's future. The cost of doing business for large department stores nationwide continued to grow, but profits and their share of the retail business were beginning to shrink. Many retailers were opening new stores in suburban malls, and there was a noticeable shift in what customers were buying. Teenagers had discovered poodle skirts and bobby socks, blue jeans and loafers. Color television debuted, and Dick Clark's *American Bandstand* swept the nation. Women appeared less interested in sophisticated styles and fashion and, instead, were buying more casual clothes. By 1955, sportswear had become the largest selling category of apparel.

Petersen's was at a crossroads along with many of the nation's 4,000 other department stores, roughly 300 of which had captured three-quarters or more of all department

By the 1950s, teenagers had discovered poodle skirts and bobby socks, blue jeans and loafers.

In the 1950s and 1960s dozens of Petersen's buying associates made the monthly trip to New York to discover new ideas, trends, and the latest brands that they brought back to the store. Some were known to meet with up to five or six vendors per hour, often for four days straight. Above left: Larry DeLookey of men's furnishings. Above right: Grace Nath of the Piece Goods section.

store business. Of those, about 75 stores were dominant and began leading the way in introducing innovative displays and more sophisticated marketing to attract new customers. Other smaller store chains did the opposite, pursuing drastic cost-cutting measures, such as closing tearooms, eliminating free delivery and doormen, and cutting back on holiday parades. Cable, Jim, and Dick Sr. weren't ready to make such sweeping cuts, but it was clear the company needed a new plan. So the timing was fortunate in 1954 when Dick Sr. was invited to join a retail interchange association, commonly known as The Scull Group. The Scull Group was a consortium of more than a dozen midsize, independent stores scattered across the country. E.H. Scull Co., an accounting and management firm, had brought the stores together after World War II to serve as a resource to one another and share information. All of the stores were roughly the same size, largely privately owned, faced similar challenges and, because they did not compete with one another, could freely exchange ideas about everything from product trends and service to sales and operations.

At that time, the two largest stores in the The Scull Group were ZCMI of Salt Lake City, and Adam Meldrum and Anderson (AM&A) of Buffalo, New York. Other stores included Loveman's in Chattanooga,

To ensure confidentiality within The Scull Group, each of the independent stores used a code number instead of a name so outsiders wouldn't be able to identify members. This was important since each store freely exchanged information about their operations. Members also visited each other's stores to see different styles and markets.

Tennessee; Porteous, Mitchell & Braun Co., a mid-market department store in Portland, Maine; Sage Allen in Hartford, Connecticut; Gottschalks, which operated in a number of western states; and The Popular of El Paso, Texas. Through the years, other stores became members, including Goudchaux's of Baton Rouge and Godchaux's of New Orleans; Harvey's in Nashville, Tennessee; and Bergner's of Peoria, Illinois.

Looking back, the von Maurs say joining The Scull Group was pivotal in helping the company survive. The group inspired many innovations the company remains known for more than half a century later, including no-interest credit cards. Jack Arth, who joined Petersen's in 1977 as a men's merchandise manager and later became president, says, "The Scull Group allowed us to see that there are many ways to run a store. We learned some things not to do by looking, listening, and analyzing the figures within the group. So we benefited from it, and others would still benefit from it today. But there is no group like it today because there is no other group of department stores that do not compete with each other. Everything is owned by just a few corporations today." Sadly, of all the department stores that were once part of The Scull Group, Von Maur is the sole survivor.

In the 1950s, hats, wigs, and hairpieces came into vogue and were prominently featured at Petersen's. The first wigs for women were pink, blue, and green and were designed to wear with swimwear. Next came human hair wigs, which were very expensive, ranging in price from $150 to $300 apiece.

Chuck von Maur

President

Chuck, born in 1930, married
Nancy, and they had two daughters,
Allison, who worked for Von Maur
for three years in management, and
Heather. Chuck spent his early years
in the office and later moved into
home furnishings and the men's
business before following a tradition
that called for the oldest brother to
become president of the company.

The Third Generation

By the mid-1950s, the von Maur family had
been in the retail business for more than 70
years. Founder C.J.'s grandsons, Chuck and
Dick, the sons of Dick Sr., were finishing
college and military service, and preparing
to join the business. As the brothers started
their careers, their father and uncles were still
making the day-to-day decisions. This gave
Chuck and Dick time to learn the business.
Chuck spent his early years in the office and
later moved into home furnishings and the
men's business. Dick began his career in
women's fashion.

In 1961, the family business was growing,
but customers' buying habits—and the
retail landscape—were changing locally and
nationally. Within a year, malls continued
to expand and the first Kmart, Target, and
Walmart stores opened, offering customers
a less-expensive shopping alternative.
Within three years, discount stores would
surpass downtown stores as the country's
No. 1 retailers.

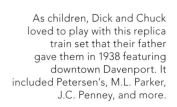

As children, Dick and Chuck
loved to play with this replica
train set that their father
gave them in 1938 featuring
downtown Davenport. It
included Petersen's, M.L. Parker,
J.C. Penney, and more.

Dick von Maur

Executive Vice President

Dick, born in 1932, married Sue, and began his career in women's fashion before eventually becoming executive vice president and secretary at Von Maur. Dick and Sue had four children: Robin, Susan, Ric, and Jim. Ric was a member of the management team for more than five years, and Jim became president in 2001.

On the left, Dick von Maur, and on the right, his older brother, Chuck.

Juniors' Sizes in Vogue

Back in Davenport, Petersen's flagship store expanded to include three adjacent store spaces, which would be used to reconfigure departments to increase sales. Toys were eliminated entirely and, in 1964, Petersen's launched The LOFT, the first store in Iowa dedicated solely to junior girls. It became an overnight success. Dick, who led the effort, recognized immediately that "Juniors" could differentiate Petersen's and breathe new life into the aging downtown store. The LOFT was a separate store for high school- and college-age girls, located adjacent to the downtown store. It featured authentic farm materials as décor, including fitting rooms that resembled horse-barn stalls. There was a soft drink machine, a telephone, a record player, and a place for girls to put their books if they stopped by after school. An ad promoting the new space invited girls to visit The LOFT, which would feature all of the latest fashions in *Seventeen* magazine, as well as "clothes and novelties for the 'in' crowd." The LOFT created such a buzz it drew executives from J.C. Penney, Sears, and Macy's. Years later, the success of The LOFT prompted Petersen's to create The Depot, a section for 7- to 14-year-old preteens with a train theme, and The Ram, a boys' department.

In 1964, The LOFT became the first store in Iowa dedicated solely to juniors clothing for girls and The Ram soon followed for boys.

One item that sold well at The LOFT in 1980 was baggy jeans. A Petersen's ad stated, "The baggy jean has arrived. The pant fits snugly at the waist and smoothly in the back. The baggy first appeared on the streets of New York during the summer of 1979, according to *Time* magazine. The customers' response from The LOFT has been exciting."

Flood and Iowa Expansion

In 1965, one year after opening The LOFT, protesters raged against U.S. involvement in the Vietnam War, the nation celebrated its first walk in space, and major changes occurred within Petersen's management team. Jim died on January 27, at 72, and Cable died just a few months later on July 10 at the age of 75. Dick Sr. became president, working with his sons, Chuck and Dick. That same year, the Great Flood of 1965 hit Davenport's downtown and Petersen's. The Mississippi River crested at a record 22.48 feet on April 28 and stayed above flood stage for 28 days. It displaced people from their homes and threatened to flood The LOFT and the popular, basement-level Tea Room,

causing both to close for two weeks. Water levels slowly rose and filled the store's elevator pit in the basement, shorting out much of the electrical system. The water took weeks to make its way down.

Three years later, in 1968, the year Martin Luther King, Jr. was assassinated and Richard Nixon was elected president, Dick Sr. was recovering from surgery. In his absence, he encouraged his sons to make their own decisions for the company. Throughout their careers, he had been a strong mentor and teacher, preparing them for the day they would take over the business. As time went on, when Chuck and Dick presented

The Great Flood of 1965 hit Davenport's downtown and Petersen's. It displaced people from their homes and threatened to flood The LOFT and the popular, basement-level Tea Room, causing both to close for two weeks.

him with serious questions about the future of the business, he was known to smile and say, "Boys, you are running the store now." He didn't want his sons to depend on him, because he knew one day they would have to function without him. That day came when, with Dick in the hospital, his sons kicked off their Iowa expansion, buying the Van Allen department store in Clinton, Iowa, on Feb. 1, 1968. The Van Allens sold their store to Petersen's, but only leased the building. The store operated for almost 20 years, but it never really took off. In March 1987, the von Maurs closed it.

Above: Van Allen Department store, Clinton, Iowa, circa 1968. The building was designed by modern American architect Louis Sullivan. He created the four-story building between 1912 and 1914, and it was considered a downtown landmark.

Buying Parker's Dubbed "Another Mistake"

In 1970, as a recession crept across the nation, Petersen's chief competitor, Parker's, was trying to sell its business after more than 50 years. When Parker's first went up for sale, there weren't any buyers. Down the street, Petersen's was struggling to expand its customer base. The von Maurs bought Parker's and spent the next year renovating the building, adding six new Montgomery escalators. Escalators had come into vogue in big city department stores decades earlier, but in Davenport, they didn't make their debut until much later. In fact, Petersen's had never had an escalator, largely because the store's layout would have required drastic alterations to accommodate it. The von Maurs hoped introducing an escalator at Parker's would greatly increase sales. They had good reason to believe it. A 1919 report showed that only 28 percent of people entering stores equipped with stairs and elevators went beyond the main floor. By the 1930s, the addition of escalators resulted in more than half of all customers traveling above or below the main floor. It was clear the farther customers went into the store, the more they would purchase.

Parker's reopened in 1971, and continued to operate under its original name. Full-page ads promoted the remodeled store. "The new Parker's is more than a store. It's a showplace." The new shoe department offered more than 40 brands and hosted a women's footwear fashion show. Despite all of the cost and time that went into the reopening, it didn't take long to realize that operating two competing stores one block apart wasn't going to work. Chuck and Dick would later say that buying Parker's had been one of their biggest mistakes. Pretty quickly, the company determined it needed to stop operating Parker's. Luckily, since they didn't own the building, they were able to get out of the lease. And, they were able to transfer the excess merchandise to the Petersen's budget store in an adjoining building, which was formerly operated by J.C. Penney.

By the 1970s, America's love affair with the suburbs and shopping malls was in full swing.

In 1972, the economy had strengthened and the Dow Jones average hit 1,000 for the first time in history. Petersen's celebrated its 100th anniversary by touting "The Sale of the Century" and the motto "Watch Us Grow!" The three-day sale in May 1972 was promoted daily in 24-page newspaper inserts, as well as on radio and television. Customers received invitations in the mail containing a "lucky number" they could bring to the store. If it matched a number in any of the departments, the customer received a discount. In-store activities included people modeling 1870 costumes. Petersen's gave away hundreds of pencils, commemorative coins, and pins and embossed napkins for the Tea Room. The Davenport newspaper reported, "The influx of shoppers downtown readily filled all available parking places in the ramps and parking lots." Dick was quoted as saying, "We expected crowds, but nothing of this magnitude. This sale, marking our 100-year history, took a full year of planning." Sale highlights included special prices on the first 1,000 women's shoes and dresses purchased, $1.99 record albums featuring Robert Goulet and David Cassidy, as well as $2.99 eight-track tapes and 50-cent single records. The store also sold ice cube trays, lawn mowers, CorningWare®, bedspreads, towels, rugs, fine china, drapes, loveseats, mattresses, tables, bedroom suites, and assorted ladies' apparel.

Looking back, the von Maurs laugh about some of their questionable ideas. On one occasion, they tried to move merchandise out of the defunct Parker's store to the Petersen's Budget Store—not via sidewalks, but by digging a tunnel through Parker's basement wall, which adjoined their bargain store. They broke through the stone wall with great effort and transferred some of the items, but the tunnel proved to be too inefficient and unsafe, so they quickly boarded it up, calling it, "Another dumb idea."

Petersen's First Mall Store

On the tail of its 100-year celebration, Petersen's opened its first mall-based store in what was essentially a strip mall. The Duck Creek Plaza store in Bettendorf, Iowa, was about one-tenth the size of the downtown Davenport store, but within four years it would double in size. Two years later, in 1974, the nation was in turmoil. Richard Nixon resigned over the Watergate break-in and the economy slid into crisis. Auto sales were off 20 percent and unemployment soared. In July of that year, Petersen's opened a much larger, two-level store at SouthPark Mall in Moline, Illinois. The $12 million mall opened with 75 stores and four major department stores, including Petersen's, Younkers, and Montgomery Ward. This was the von Maurs' first significant branch store

in a suburban shopping center. But it didn't come without a struggle. This must have felt like déjà vu. After all, the family's first major bump in the road came in Moline in 1929 when they bought Fisk and Loosley. Now, General Growth Properties, the SouthPark Mall developer, was rebuffing offers to make Petersen's one of the anchor tenants. The von Maurs knew that Younkers owned a percentage of General Growth Properties, and they feared the Iowa-based competitor would block their entry. The von Maurs put an option on land abutting the mall and told developers that, if forced to, they would open a freestanding store. That prompted the developers to approve Petersen's as one of the main anchor stores at SouthPark Mall.

Above: Petersen's opened SouthPark Mall in Moline, Illinois, on Feb. 27, 1974. It was the von Maurs' first significant branch store in a suburban shopping center.

100-Year Anniversary Song

Take me down to Ole Petersen's,
Take me down to the Sale,
Buy me some pillows and lollipops,
I'm so happy I'll do a big hop.
So it's root, root, root for a Century,
A hundred years of true fun,
And it's 1-2-3- days that's all,
And we'll all have a ball.

Take me back for a Century,
Take me back for a while,
Selling will be such a great delight,
You can sell everything in your sight.
So be kind and courteous tomorrow,
For we have an honor to uphold,
For it's smile, smile, smile, that is all,
And we'll feel ten feet tall.

Take me down to Ole Petersen's,
Down where the bargains are neat,
And shopping is something for everyone,
And millions of people will have fun, fun, fun.
So take me down to the basement,
And all the way up to four,
Just be certain to buy all the bargains,
Before they close the door.

Sung by Chuck and Dick to the tune of
"Take Me Out to the Ball Game."

chapter 5

LAWSUITS, FIRES, AND BUYOUTS

By the mid-1970s, in an age of conglomerates and headline-grabbing corporate takeovers, Petersen's had quietly become Iowa's largest independent department store chain. In nearly every way, Petersen's had one foot in the traditional world of downtown retailing and a second foot in the new world of suburban malls. In 1974, a Minnesota developer announced plans to build Valley West Mall in Des Moines, Iowa, in what was currently a cornfield. The question was: would customers really flock to a mall in an unpopulated area on the outskirts of town? It didn't help that from the start the project was embroiled in controversy and legal battles. Des Moines-based Meredith Corporation, best known for publishing two of America's

most popular magazines, *Better Homes and Gardens* and *Ladies' Home Journal*, objected to the mall site. They had planned to build Meredith's corporate headquarters next door and were concerned the new mall would interfere. After a number of months, Meredith Corporation withdrew its complaint, and the mall project was back on track. Despite the uncertainty, the von Maurs signed the lease, securing a place as one of the mall's premier anchor stores.

No sooner was the ink dry on the mall lease than Dayton Hudson Corporation filed a multimillion dollar lawsuit against Valley West Des Moines Shopping Center, Inc., claiming it had been promised the spot

Above: On Aug. 4, 1975, Petersen's opened a new store in Valley West Mall in Des Moines. The store put a significant strain on the company's finances in its early days. (Architectural Rendering)

the new Petersen's store would occupy. As part of the lawsuit, Dayton Hudson sought an injunction to halt construction on the $22 million shopping center project. But it quickly became clear the lawsuit had no merit. So, in short order, the small company from Davenport prevailed. With the legal battle behind them, the von Maurs began to address other concerns. Building a new store, as opposed to taking over an existing store space, was expensive, and they had not secured all the necessary financing. Fortunately, a local bank stepped forward to help solidify the financing. Still, the lawsuit had put the project behind schedule. J.C. Penney, the third anchor store with Petersen's and Brandeis, refused to sign a lease until the legal matter was resolved. That meant Valley West Mall opened on Aug. 4, 1975, with only 20 stores and a single anchor store, Brandeis, of Omaha, Nebraska. It would be almost a year before the mall held its grand opening, on July 28, 1976, with Petersen's and 40 more specialty stores in place.

From the start, it was clear Des Moines customers were more excited about having a new Brandeis store than Petersen's. There was no denying the fact that the Brandeis name was better recognized among retail shoppers, and this was the retailer's first store outside its home state of Nebraska. "With sales last year of nearly $75 million and assets of $48 million, Brandeis brings considerable clout to Des Moines," the *Des Moines Register* reported on July 27, 1975, in one of a series of stories about the retailer. "It owns stock in the same buying group as do many other large retailers, such as Dayton Hudson Corp. Thus, it can draw on some 15,000 sources in 63 countries to bring merchandise to Des Moines."

The *Register* went on to write that Brandeis would be a "feisty competitor for Younkers Brothers, Inc.," a company that had $106 million in sales that same year. The Iowa-based Younkers had long dominated the Des Moines market. Brandeis knew this and to gain favor with local customers, it built a 5,000-square-foot auditorium in its new Des Moines store that could be used for free by local, charitable, and nonprofit groups. Almost as a footnote, the *Register* reported that Petersen's, "a small but aggressive Davenport company," would also be in the mall. Few believed the new Petersen's would be able to compete on the same level as Brandeis and Younkers.

Pictured here: the Brandeis Omaha store. In 1975, Brandeis opened its first store outside its home state of Nebraska when it entered Valley West Mall in Des Moines, alongside Younkers and Petersen's.

A Popular Spot for Lunch

Shopping and eating at Petersen's department store was a long-standing tradition. Many planned their shopping day to include a visit to the Tea Room, and later Petersen's Pantry, where they could get food that was prepared fresh daily, including an olive nut spread sandwich.

Olive Nut Spread

One of the most popular items on the downtown store's menu was Olive Nut Spread. Here's the secret recipe!

¾ cup softened cream cheese

½ cup mayonnaise

½ cup chopped pecans

1 cup stuffed green olives, chopped

2 tablespoons liquid from the olives to moisten as needed

Dash of black pepper

Mix well

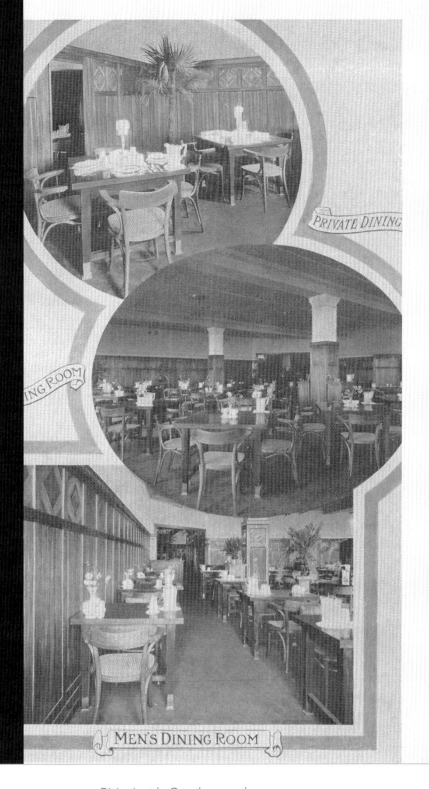

Dining in style: Over the years, the stores provided many opportunities for customers to dine together. These photos are circa 1887-1912 from the original Harned & Von Maur store.

Down but Not Out

Petersen's was quickly discovering what it was like to play in the big leagues. The new store was putting a significant strain on the company's finances, and things were about to get worse. Only a handful of people attended a black-tie event hosted by the mall developer the night before the Petersen's grand opening. And when the store opened the next day, it only vaguely resembled a Petersen's store. There were very few fixtures, tables, or counters because the manufacturer didn't deliver them on time. Instead, Petersen's associates had to decorate the store with cardboard boxes covered with tablecloths. "We only had a handful of customers anyway. It was a terrible beginning," Dick recalls. "Thank goodness for our dedicated employees. They hung in there." Few people knew it at the time, but sales were so thin in Des Moines that nearly everyone back at headquarters feared the slow start might bring down the company.

Younkers executives knew the Petersen's store at Valley West was not doing well and quietly approached the retailer about buying the store for the depreciated assets on the books. Leaders of both companies held a series

Above: Younker's flagship store in downtown Des Moines. Younkers, a long-established Iowa company founded in 1874, was known as the place to shop.

(Photo courtesy of the *Des Moines Register*)

of secret meetings in old motels in Moline, because neither wanted it known that they were discussing a possible sale. "Younkers put on quite a snow job that they would be helping us out by buying our business," Dick remembers. "Always 'helping' was their ploy." The final meeting about the sale was at a private home in Des Moines. As the brothers drove to the meeting, they were still undecided about selling. "We got out of the car and walked up the sidewalk, and Chuck said, 'Dick, they are not going to steal it. We are going to ask well more than the depreciated asset value of the store.' And Dick said, 'We are not going to sell it, period.'"

When the brothers approached the house, the door opened and two maids greeted them with cookies, coffee, and lemonade. Once the von Maurs told the Younkers executives that they would not sell the Des Moines store, "the cookies and coffee were taken away and the lemonade went sour," Dick recalls. "You should have seen their reaction when we said 'No.' Their jaws dropped and the meeting was over." Driving home, Chuck and Dick wondered if they had made a significant mistake. "It was our darkest times when that store struggled," Chuck says. "Younkers was the store in Des Moines. Plus, our location was so remote to the Des Moines community. We didn't know if we had done the right thing."

The company's fight to keep the store afloat continued for months and played out before the public. At one point, the *Des Moines Register* published an article speculating that Petersen's would sell its Des Moines store. That prompted Petersen's to place an ad in the *Register* that stated, "Thank you Des Moines for making Valley West our fastest-growing store." Two years after opening, sales at the Des Moines store were slowly improving. But the good news was tempered on Nov. 5, 1978, when a fire destroyed the Younkers store at Merle Hay Mall, killing 10 employees. The fire occurred early on a Sunday morning before the store had opened. It caused an estimated $20 million in damage and would change the course of history for Younkers.

On the day of the fire, Jack Arth, who had joined the von Maurs' management team just a year earlier, and Dick were on the same airplane as the Younkers president. They were traveling to New York on a buying trip. "I'll never forget that day because while we were on the plane none of us knew what had happened," Arth says. "We were in New York when Chuck called us with the news. Business aside, it was a true tragedy." It took investigators months to determine that faulty wiring had caused what would become known as the worst fire in Des Moines' history. During the investigation, the

Jack Arth

A New Team Member

Jack Arth worked at Stix, Baer, and Fuller in St. Louis before joining Petersen's in 1977. Stix was recognized as the leading high-end fashion store in the St. Louis metropolitan area. Associated Dry Goods had recently purchased it, so Arth was no longer certain he would have a job. When Chuck reached out to him, Arth recalls thinking, "What's Petersen's, and who are the von Maurs?" After working for Stix for 22 years, Arth wasn't sure he wanted to move to a company that had a much smaller volume. "But on the positive side," Arth says, "I was amazed at the level of customer service, and I felt an immediate chemistry with Dick and Chuck." Within a decade, Arth would become president of the company.

Younkers store at Merle Hay Mall remained closed. Younkers had 28 stores in five states, but the fire's impact proved to be too much for the company's bottom line. In 1979, Younkers announced it would sell to Equitable of Iowa insurance company for $72.2 million. "As competitive as we had been with Younkers, we never wanted to benefit from someone else's tragedy," Chuck said. "This was a very sad and difficult situation."

Over the next 30 years, ownership of Younkers changed again and again, reflecting a larger transformation within the nation's retail industry. In an interesting twist, Younkers purchased Brandeis in 1987. Nearly a decade later, in 1996, Proffitt's, Inc. acquired Younkers, and two years later merged with Saks Fifth Avenue to form Saks Inc. Through all of these transitions, Von Maur stayed the course as an independent, family-owned department store. "We had made mistakes along the way with the Des Moines store, but by 1996 it was our largest volume store," Arth says. "It bailed us out of some bumps in the road."

The economy in Davenport and the greater Quad Cities in the early 1980s was at an all-time low during the Farm Crisis. John Deere & Co., the area's leading employer, cut employment nearly in half, to about 9,000 from a peak of 16,840 in 1980. Five years later, International Harvester closed a plant in nearby Rock Island, Illinois, and two years later, Caterpillar, known as the world's largest maker of construction equipment, closed its Davenport plant. All told, more than 35,000 jobs were lost. Looking back, Dick says, "Building the Des Moines store turned out to be one of our luckiest decisions. The store gave us the stability our company needed to remain solvent during those years."

New Faces and Spaces

In the midst of the West Des Moines store startup, Petersen's added a new men's merchandise manager to its management team. The von Maur brothers had heard about Jack Arth, a well-respected men's merchandise buyer at Stix, Baer, and Fuller in the St. Louis metropolitan area.

A kind, but disciplined and demanding merchant, Arth joined the company in 1977 and initially reported to Chuck, who was the men's merchandise manager and also oversaw home goods. In short order, the von Maur brothers recognized Arth's leadership skills and urged him to expand his retail knowledge by learning more about women's fashion. "I had to rely entirely on them at first because I had never worked in women's merchandise," Arth says. "I also didn't know much about running stores. I was more of a merchant." Dick mentored Arth about women's wear and shoes, and Chuck taught him about home goods. Arth was steeped in the company's philosophies of customer service, professionalism, and business etiquette. As trust grew among the men, Arth's responsibilities broadened. "I didn't realize what their end goal was," says Arth, who a

The drapery department sold custom-made draperies to banks, homes, offices, dinner clubs, and more.

decade later became the first person outside the von Maur family to become president. "They were like my brothers." The irony, Arth says, is that in today's retail world he likely would never have gotten an interview with the company or any other major retailer. "I didn't have a college degree," he says. "Everything I had learned, I learned on the floor selling merchandise. Honestly, I've often thought about how quickly things have changed. In today's world, I would be lucky to get an interview at Walmart with the education I had." Over the years, Petersen's employed many associates who had never been to college. "We couldn't have cared less if our employees had college degrees—then or now," Dick says.

By 1979, the company's continued success prompted another leap. When Montgomery Ward pulled out of Muscatine Mall in Iowa, Petersen's took its place, joining anchor stores Walmart and J.C. Penney. A Chicago architect helped redesign the Muscatine store, creating "lifestyle zones," or what many called boutiques in which each department assumed a different identity. High walls and other barriers separated the departments. If customers stood in the children's department, they may not have been able to see over the wall to the women's section or shoe section. Dividing departments was common for most department stores during this era. On

Aug. 24, 1979, Petersen's opened in the Muscatine Mall with a new look and a celebration theme of "We love you, Muscatine." The store incorporated warm tones, with natural wood, and indirect lighting. Petersen's now had stores in the Quad Cities, Clinton, Des Moines, and Muscatine.

The company also remodeled its flagship Davenport downtown store in an effort to compete against the growing number of mall stores. Some aspects of the store were consolidated and others eliminated, including the candy department, which had been a mainstay for decades. Some distinctions remained. The store still featured a photography studio, and customers continued to flock to the Tea Room, which served up favorites such as hot fudge sundaes, waffles, and sandwiches. At the end of 1979, while Jimmy Carter was in the White House,

Store Security

Eye in the Sky

Over the years, the von Maurs have faced many security issues. In the early days, there were no cameras to keep an eye on shoppers. On one occasion, the von Maurs knew someone was stealing from the jewelry department. They hired a security guard who climbed high above the store's false ceiling before customers arrived for the day. He cut a peephole over the jewelry counter where he crouched, peering through the hole for hours. The von Maurs even wired a telephone into the ceiling in case he needed to call downstairs. "The poor guy was up there all day and night," Chuck remembered. The store closed at 5 p.m. and by 5:05 p.m. the man had identified the person who was stealing. "The funny part is that when he came in to debrief us, his eye was redder than a cranberry and all puffed up," Chuck says. "He had been peering through that hole for way too long."

The Man in the Box

During the 1960s, the von Maur's downtown store was large and extended across many buildings. That made it difficult to keep tabs on all of the merchandise and the cash moving through dozens of registers. One day, the von Maurs realized something was amiss in the men's department, which was adjacent to linens and domestics. The domestics department often had inventory that had to be brought onto the floor in large boxes and unloaded. The von Maurs decided to put a man inside a large pillow box. They cut a small peephole in the side of the box, loaded the man into it and then brought him into domestics on a dolly. They faced the peephole toward the men's department. About 15 minutes before the store closed, the man in the box saw someone taking money, jumped out of the box and shouted, "Don't move." As the story goes, store associates later laughed and said the incident nearly gave them a heart attack.

In the 1970s, Petersen's lacked the sophisticated look that would become a hallmark of the company in the coming years.

the national economy began to sputter. There was double-digit inflation, gasoline prices were well over a dollar a gallon, and the dollar had weakened abroad. By the 1980s, Iowa and the nation had entered a recession. Iowa's agricultural industry was flagging, putting a strain on farmers, agriculturally focused businesses, banks, and dozens of the Midwest's downtown stores.

Four New Locations in a Year

While many store chains were looking to downsize or putting a hold on their expansions, Petersen's did quite the opposite. In 1980, Brandeis announced plans to open a store at Westdale, a new mall in Cedar Rapids, Iowa, the state's second largest city. During construction, Brandeis withdrew its commitment, leaving an opening for a new Petersen's store. In September 1980, Petersen's opened, joining Montgomery Ward, J.C. Penney, and Younkers as anchors, along with 120 other specialty stores.

One year later, the von Maurs were still shopping for new locations. In 1981, developers wanted to expand NorthPark Mall in Davenport to add Petersen's, but the Davenport City Council had to approve the changes. This was the von Maur's hometown, a place where they had lived and operated their family business for almost a century. They anticipated the city approval process would go smoothly. Everyone knew the downtown was suffering, but what the von Maurs didn't foresee was that the City Council would be reluctant to do anything that would give Petersen's an incentive to close their flagship downtown store and move to the mall. "We didn't think it was fair they wouldn't approve a local company, but instead earlier they had approved J.C. Penney's, Younkers, and Wards over us," Dick says. The council ultimately did approve the expansion, and Petersen's opened a store at NorthPark Mall on Sept. 3, 1981. The von Maurs say the controversy served as a reminder that even successful companies sometimes have to fight for their futures in their own backyards.

For nearly a century, shopping downtown had been an all-day affair that included stopping by the candy counter, having a family photo taken, shopping for a new Sunday outfit, or having lunch or tea.

Above: The original soda fountain at Harned & Von Maur (1887 – 1912).

On Sept. 6, 1980, Petersen's opened its
Westdale Mall location in Cedar Rapids, Iowa,
as shown in this early rendering.

That same year, it became clear Killian's, a well-established, well-respected store in Cedar Rapids, Iowa, was struggling. They had operated a popular downtown store in Cedar Rapids since the early 1900s and had added locations at Lindale Mall in Cedar Rapids and Sycamore Mall in Iowa City. When Killian's reluctantly put the Lindale and Sycamore stores up for sale, the von Maurs eagerly purchased them and opened new stores in the locations on Oct. 7, 1981.

Petersen's had one more failed Iowa department store in its sights. The company hired a New York consultant to appraise the recently closed Roshek's department store in Dubuque. J.J. Roshek founded the nine-story store, and at one time, Roshek's claimed to be Iowa's largest department store. The consultant looked the store over while the brothers anxiously awaited his opinion. As he boarded the airplane to leave, he said, "That is the finest mausoleum I have ever seen. It's a morgue." Chuck says the consultant

"really saved us on that one. We might have bought it otherwise. This was one mistake we didn't make."

By the time the holiday season arrived in 1981, Petersen's was operating a dozen stores in Iowa and Illinois, employing more than 1,200 people. A holiday message to associates acknowledged that the past year had been the most dramatic growth year in the company's history. Building a new store and adding two more had put an enormous strain on the company and its associates. Amidst the growth, rumors occasionally surfaced that Petersen's, like many retailers nationwide, was being bought out. The brothers routinely dismissed such thoughts. "You keep it a family business as long as you have an interest in running it and seeing that it remains exciting and creative," Chuck told the *Quad City Times* on March 15, 1981. He went on to say that the company had been offering strong service and quality merchandise for decades. "We have survived by doing our own thing. We've been putting up with new competition for more than 100 years."

Above: Killian's Department Store, Cedar Rapids, Iowa

Right: The Roshek building in Dubuque, Iowa

Staff gathered on the balcony of the downtown Davenport store in 1981 to celebrate the holidays.

chapter 6

THINKING OUTSIDE
THE SHOEBOX

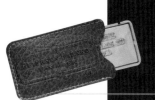

(1982-1985)

The von Maurs had opened nine stores in 15 years. While the company had taken some risks by moving to the cornfields of Des Moines, going head to head with Younkers and Brandeis, and unveiling a new Juniors store, little else had changed. Essentially, the company was using the same business model founder C.J. and his three sons had created in the early 1900s. But over the next few years, nearly everything the von Maurs believed to be absolutes within their department stores would be reexamined, and in many cases, retooled. They would turn their corporate culture upside down, introduce an interest-free customer charge card, and walk away from the home goods business. Petersen's also expanded its selection of fashion and accessories, while simultaneously ushering in

a dramatically different look for all of their stores. "Looking back, I would argue that it would be hard to accomplish this type of thing in this day and age," says Jack Arth, Von Maur president from 1989 to 1998. "Those were different times. The von Maurs literally remade their company during the 1980s."

It was 1984, and the Midwest was still reeling from the Farm Crisis. For the third year in a row, the value of farmland dropped, with the largest declines in the nation recorded in Iowa and Nebraska. This was bad news for farmers and for agricultural-related industries, which were a staple in communities throughout Iowa and Illinois. It also meant fewer dollars were finding their way into retail stores. Nationally, the country was in a recession. Petersen's

Above: A Petersen's charga-plate—the predecessor to today's credit cards.

From left, Dick Sr. and his sons, Chuck
and Dick, standing in front of their
Davenport store, circa 1970.

needed an infusion of new ideas. A few times a year, the von Maurs and Arth still traveled to different parts of the country to visit other retailers in The Scull Group. One of those stores was Goudchaux's in Baton Rouge, Louisiana, which had introduced interest-free credit and was doing the largest volume per square foot of any single department store in the country. The von Maurs had debated the issue of extending interest-free credit for several years, consulting bankers and accountants who unequivocally told them not to do it. But the von Maurs knew customers loved Goudchaux's (and its acquired Maison Blanche) in part because it offered the best services. The Louisiana economy was struggling, savings and loans were collapsing, and some retail titans were sliding into bankruptcy. Through it all Goudchaux-Maison Blanche thrived. At its peak, the retailer had 24 stores with 640,000 customer charge accounts, making it the largest family-owned department store group in the country. The von Maurs saw this success and remembered their pledge to implement one good idea a year from fellow independent stores in The Scull Group. Chuck and Dick believed the interest-free charge account was that new idea. They also realized this was not a change they could make lightly. "We knew our accountants would think this was the craziest—and riskiest—idea yet," Chuck says.

Our Only Interest Is You

The issue of extending some type of credit to customers was nothing new to the company. As early as 1927, Harned & Von Maur sent personal recommendation cards to customers authorizing them to open a credit account. In 1938, as part of the 10-year merger celebration, the store extended credit to customers through Charga-plates—the predecessor to today's credit cards. Early on, these took the form of a coin disk, about the size of a quarter, embossed with a customer's name and address. Each disk, and later metal plates, had two to three notches unique to each customer. After placing a disk in an imprinting machine, the clerk had to "call up the charge" to the credit office. Someone in the credit department would check the person's account and decide whether he or she could use credit. If approved, the credit department could send an electrical signal to the machine, allowing the charge. The Petersen's 1938 ad stated, "No need to state your name or address, no need to waste time spelling, simply hand your Petersen Charga-plate to the salesperson for instant service."

The above medallion was the original token used to identify customers for credit. It preceded the charga-plate and credit cards.

R.H. HARNED, PRESIDENT.   C.J. VON MAUR, VICE PRESIDENT.   C.G. VON MAUR, SECY.   H.W. VON MAUR, TREAS.

Harned & Von Maur
(INCORPORATED)
DEPARTMENT STORE
§
WHOLESALE AND RETAIL
NEW YORK OFFICE 23 EAST 26TH ST.

Davenport, Iowa.

April 1, 1927.

DIRECTORS
R.H. HARNED
C.J. VON MAUR
C.G. VON MAUR
H.W. VON MAUR
R.G. VON MAUR
C.C. CESSNA
R.R. WALN

Miss Betty Monn,
Davenport, Iowa.

Dear Madam:-

There are more than 15,000 Tri-City people who enjoy the convenience of a charge account here, at Harned & Von Maur's.

We looked for your name among them but find that you are not now availing yourself of this convenience, and it is to extend to you an invitation to do so, that we are writing this letter.

Enclosed is a personal recommendation card. Just present it to the salesperson from whom you make your purchase and an account will immediately be opened for you. It will not even be necessary for you to go to our credit office.

You will find that we appreciate your patronage. This appreciation is reflected in the courteous service of our salespeople; in the care we exercise in seeing that all goods offered you measure up to our strict standard of quality; in our eagerness to adjust any cause of dissatisfaction due to faulty merchandise or service and in our well-known policy of never permitting ourselves to be undersold by any other Tri-City store.

We believe that you will like trading at Harned & Von Maur's and we certainly extend you the most cordial invitation to come in the next time you're downtown and open an account.

Yours truly,

HARNED & VON MAUR

R.H. Harned

President.

MR. W. K. CRANDELL
CREDIT MANAGER
HARNED & VON MAUR

I HAVE PERSONALLY INVITED

Miss Betty Monn
MRS.

TO OPEN AN ACCOUNT HERE

R.H. Harned
PRES.

This 1927 letter of credit and "personal recommendation card" was extended to Harned & Von Maur customers, inviting them to open a charge account.

A Petersen's credit employee sits at a rolling desk with a mounted telephone. Before a customer's purchase could be charged, sales associates had to "call up" to the credit department so the customer's account could be reviewed.

When World War II broke out, the use of credit changed across the nation. Travel and buying curtailed and the government put controls on credit. It wasn't until the 1950s that credit began to make a comeback in the form of Diner's Club cards and the introduction of American Express. By 1983, most retailers were expanding their lucrative credit card programs, offering customers more sophisticated charge account options. Petersen's customers could sign up for a revolving charge account or an option account. In either case, customers who didn't pay off their balance within 30 days were charged interest as high as 20 percent on unpaid balances. Some of the nation's largest retailers were making more money off interest income than merchandise sales.

The von Maurs knew it would be tough to convince their accountants that an interest-free credit card was a wise move. "But we wanted to do it because we thought it was the right thing to do," Dick says. "That was really the bottom line. We didn't like the idea of charging our customers that kind of interest." In 1984, the von Maurs and Arth met with their accountants. They thought they were meeting one-on-one with a senior partner; instead they were greeted by a roomful of people. "It felt like they brought every member of their firm," Arth says. "I think they all came to see if these two von Maur boys were nuts. They must have thought they had to walk away from all of this interest income and take the risk to try to sell more goods to make up for it." A senior accounting partner detailed the increased volume of merchandise Petersen's would have to sell, adding, "There is no way you can do this." In the end, the accounting firm wouldn't sign off on the idea. "They thought it was absolute suicide," Arth recalls. The meeting ended and the von Maurs were left to contemplate the future. By adopting the program, they would sacrifice lucrative interest income, but they also believed it would increase customer loyalty. "I think it was their desire to survive that guided them in making that decision," Arth says. "If they did everything the big retailers did, then they wouldn't survive because they were the little guy. It was David versus Goliath. Our volume was nothing compared to the big stores."

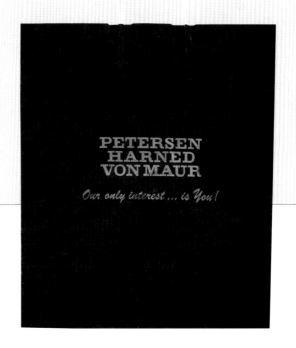

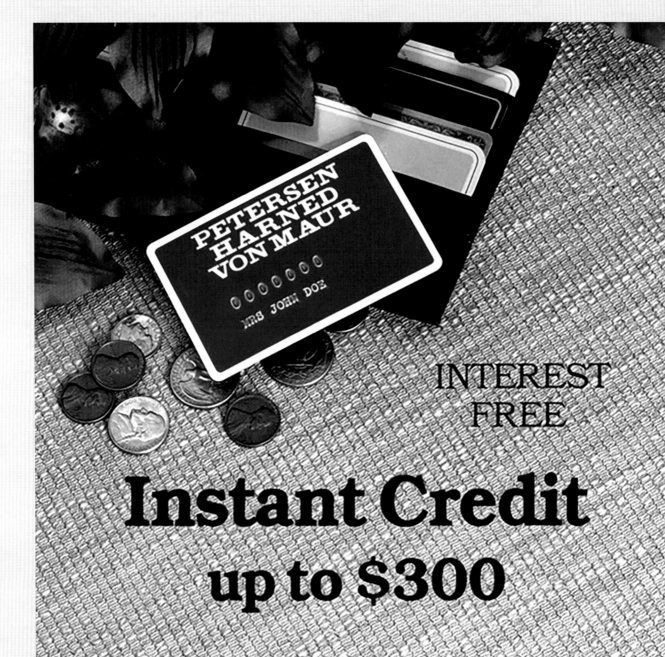

INTEREST FREE

Instant Credit up to $300

With A Photo I.D. And MasterCard or VISA

Subject To Our Credit Terms

A March 28, 1985, Petersen's flyer highlights its new interest-free charge program. "With a Petersen's Interest-Free Charge Account, you can spread your monthly payments over several months and pay no interest or annual fee. It's a fact: Over a one-year period, you would pay $99 in finance charges on an average monthly balance of $500, using a conventional revolving charge plan. (Interest charge based on 19.8 annual percentage rate.) Petersen's interest-free charge account costs nothing. Our only interest is you!"

That same year, Petersen's introduced interest-free credit, creating an advertising campaign titled, "Our Only Interest Is You." Dick's son, Jim, who became company president in 2001, says the program has become synonymous with Von Maur. Customers pay no interest, finance charge, or monthly or annual fee, whether they pay their total account balance each month or spread payments over several months. By the mid-1990s, nearly 60 percent of Petersen's sales were charged on the store's card, compared to an industry average of 40 percent. Those percentages eroded in the coming years for all retailers, in part because credit card companies began offering cash back and mileage incentives, prompting fewer people to use store credit cards. But the percentage of Von Maur customers who use the retailer's credit card is still much higher than that of its competitors. "The decision to offer interest-free credit is another one of the reasons we're still here as a company," Arth says. "It goes back to integrity. If the customers feel like they are going to benefit, then they will be more loyal. And that's how our customers feel about the no-interest charge card." Jim agrees, saying that while other retail chains have offered no-interest credit cards from time to time, they have never stayed with the program. "It's costly," he says. "It would be easier to charge interest. We don't do that, because we know our interest-free program is another big reason customers come back."

Dick Sr. pictured circa 1920

In Memoriam

In December 1985, Dick Sr. died at the age of 89. "We lost the country's best merchant and our best friend," his son, Dick, said, who along with his brother, Chuck, took over the family business.

chapter 7

IT'S CURTAINS FOR HOME GOODS

Understated elegance is a phrase many use to describe the Von Maur stores and the family members who run them. With Chuck and Dick stepping up to lead the company in 1986, the *Des Moines Register* published an article featuring the brothers. Chuck had just been named president and Dick was executive vice president and secretary. Titles aside, they ran the company in tandem. "The brothers who make the operation go, keep a low profile. They pride themselves on being on top of fashion trends, a critical skill in their business," the article stated. "…They're Chuck and Dick to friends. They're known for having a good sense of humor."

During the interview, Chuck said his brother was such an expert on the department store business that he had written a book on the subject. Chuck took a hardbound copy from a bookshelf and handed it to the reporter. "The title was impressive, something like, 'All I Know About the Retail Business,' by Dick," the article stated. "But the pages, a couple hundred or more, were blank. Both enjoyed the humor."

Like the three von Maur brothers a generation earlier, Chuck and Dick prided themselves on working well together and spending time on the sales floor to keep in touch with customers and associates. "We're in a business of constant change," Chuck told the *Register*. "Unless we listen to people, we may not be in tune with where to take the business."

The furniture department at the downtown
Davenport store, circa 1970.

The linens and domestics department in
the downtown Davenport store, circa 1970.

One of the first things the brothers did was to promote Jack Arth to company-wide executive vice president and general manager. They admired Arth and wanted another merchant in top management to help make significant decisions. Together, the three debated their first looming decision: whether to remodel the Duck Creek Plaza store, which was entering its 10th year. As they discussed Duck Creek, the conversation quickly turned to the design of all of their stores. Most of the store designs had followed the lead of their flagship downtown store, which featured lifestyle zones—a maze-like configuration of departments separated by high walls. The zones were popular in the 1980s, but they made it difficult for customers to travel from one department to the next.

Petersen's Duck Creek store was different. It had an open floor plan customers really liked. One day, Jack's wife, Joyce, made an offhanded comment about whether anyone had considered building all of their stores with an open floor plan like Duck Creek. Without walls, customers could see where they were going and easily find the next department. It was an intriguing idea. The brothers and Arth took the idea to their architect, who vehemently opposed it. The von Maurs were taken aback; after all, this was a highly respected Chicago architect whose company had worked with Petersen's

for years. They loved his past designs, but they wanted something more, something that would set them apart from the competition. Arth recalls the architect balked, saying, "If I do that you won't look like a department store, you'll look like a discount store. In fact, if you want to go that way, I'm not your man. I'll go back to Chicago, and you can find someone else." He got up from the table, packed his briefcase, and left. "Dick and I were kind of stunned," Arth recalls. "We had upset this guy, and all we were trying to do is what our customers told us they wanted."

Unsure what to do, the von Maurs and Arth visited a number of national retailers from coast to coast. They returned full of energy and ideas, ready to implement a new vision. They wanted to create stores with no interior walls, wide-open spaces, very little signage, no mannequins, and a softer spotlighting system instead of large, glaring commercial fluorescent lighting used in most department stores of the day. "The brothers had a talent for looking at different stores around the nation and using a small piece from here and there to create their own unique formula," Arth says.

During their travels, the brothers had an "aha" moment when they realized they could be selling a lot more shoes. Petersen's had given up control of its shoe department

For more than four decades at Petersen's downtown Davenport store, shoppers would pause when they heard a series of melodic "dings" overhead. This call system was often used to page key personnel. At the store, one "ding" meant someone was trying to contact Chuck, and three "dings" was for Dick.

years ago to International Shoe Company in St. Louis, then the largest shoe manufacturer in the nation. "The further we got into this shoe thing, the more it boggled our minds," Arth says. "We realized we needed to take back control of our shoe departments and make them a much larger part of our business. It was clear that while home goods brought in some customers, shoes were an even larger draw."

The von Maurs had the vision, but who was going to redesign the stores? They called Fred Ebeling, a local architect who had completed a few smaller projects for Petersen's. Dick asked Ebeling how many stores he had designed in his career. Ebeling mentioned a few small stores in Davenport. Ebeling recalled, "Dick loved to put a bead on a person, so he said, 'Let me be more specific, How many department stores have you designed?' I swallowed and told him, 'None.' And he said, 'Good. That is the right answer. That is what we are looking for. You're our man.'"

Goodbye Home Goods

In order to expand Petersen's shoe department, the company had to streamline other merchandise. Defying yet another department store trend, the retailer eliminated home goods so it could focus on fashion, shoes, and accessories. This was risky.

Petersen's had built a reputation for home goods that accounted for about 15 percent of sales. Some of their most popular home goods were custom items, such as draperies, slipcovers, and fabric window shades. There was a good chance loyal customers would be upset by the change. "All of these things were going through Chuck's and Dick's minds, but they just kept coming back to the fact that it would be a key differentiator among the competition," Arth says. All three agreed the key to expanding into new and larger markets was to offer customers something other stores lacked. From the beginning, Arth says, the brothers kept asking, "'How do we become the customer's favorite store?' and 'Why would vendors want to sell to our company instead of the others?' They let those questions guide their changes."

In the spring of 1986, Petersen's embarked on an aggressive, two-year remodeling and updating program. "We realized if we were going to move into shopping centers, we were going to be up against bigger competition," says Chuck. "We had to concentrate on fewer things: men's, women's and children's apparel, accessories, shoes, and, most important, customer service."

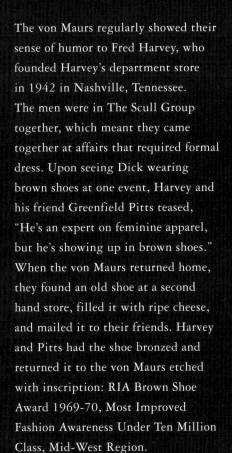

The von Maurs regularly showed their sense of humor to Fred Harvey, who founded Harvey's department store in 1942 in Nashville, Tennessee. The men were in The Scull Group together, which meant they came together at affairs that required formal dress. Upon seeing Dick wearing brown shoes at one event, Harvey and his friend Greenfield Pitts teased, "He's an expert on feminine apparel, but he's showing up in brown shoes." When the von Maurs returned home, they found an old shoe at a second hand store, filled it with ripe cheese, and mailed it to their friends. Harvey and Pitts had the shoe bronzed and returned it to the von Maurs etched with inscription: RIA Brown Shoe Award 1969-70, Most Improved Fashion Awareness Under Ten Million Class, Mid-West Region.

In the 1980s, the von Maurs eliminated home goods to make room for expanded fashion apparel and shoe departments.

chapter 8

NEW DAY DAWNS AS DOWNTOWN STORE CLOSES

It was the mid-1980s, and the nation's economy continued to expand under President Ronald Reagan. Coca-Cola shocked the nation when it announced plans to do away with its classic formula and launch a new recipe. The soft drink giant wasn't the only company tinkering with a winning formula. The von Maurs announced they would close their 114-year-old flagship store in downtown Davenport, which had been in decline for years. This was a difficult decision; the store had been the company's crown jewel for decades and had provided stability for a downtown still struggling to recover from the Farm Crisis. But Chuck and Dick believed the downtown would only continue to slip as people's shopping habits continued to change.

"It's a blow, but it's not fatal," Davenport Mayor Thomas Hart told the *Quad City Times* on Aug. 9, 1986. "They are a strong corporate citizen in Davenport, the Quad Cities, and Iowa, and will continue to be. I'm sure the decision they've made is more painful for them than anybody." Dick agreed, telling the newspaper, "Chuck and I have done enough grieving for everyone over this. It's been our life." For weeks, the local newspaper ran articles about the closing. Bill Wundrum, a longtime writer for the *Quad City Times,* penned a column the day the closure was announced. Its headline stated, "They keep on falling: And now, even Gilbralter." He wrote, "Just like they always said, 'There'll always be Petersen's downtown. There just had to be

Parking downtown was becoming more of a
challenge for Petersen's customers. Meters
meant it was more expensive to park there
than at the new malls, and delivery trucks often
clogged the narrow downtown streets.

Petersen's downtown. Downtown without Pete's would be like Davenport without the Mississippi River.' Other dominoes could fall in half-empty blocks of vacant Second Street storefronts. But not Petersen's with its polished brass nameplates and revolving doors. Petersen's was downtown Davenport's Gilbralter at Second and Main...I strolled this morning into the cavernous store after getting the sad news. I remembered my childhood, and my children's childhood, of a half-block of Christmas windows, a joy of dancing chipmunks and merry mice. Just like Marshall Field's in Chicago. Maybe even better. I counted only three customers on the whole main floor at mid-morning. Every employee looked as if they were at a funeral."

On October 9, the final day of business, a driving rain kept many customers away. The majority of the store was quiet, but people crowded into Petersen's Pantry to experience "lunch at Pete's" one last time. It was difficult for the von Maurs and their customers to acknowledge that the romantic era of downtown shopping was coming to an end. Gone were the days when families dressed up to take a trip downtown, first by horse and buggy, later by trolley, and now by car or city bus. For nearly a century, shopping downtown had been something special. Sometimes it was an all-day affair that included stopping by the candy counter, having a family photo taken, shopping for a new Sunday outfit, or having lunch or tea with family and friends.

On Oct. 9, 1986, Petersen's closed its flagship store in downtown Davenport.

Although the decision was difficult, the von Maurs knew they had fought longer than many to hold onto their downtown store. As early as the 1950s and 1960s, downtowns across the country were beginning to show signs of age and neglect. Department stores were disappearing even in large cities such as Boston, Philadelphia, and New York City. Conditions only worsened over the next two decades, as more people moved out to the suburbs and fewer people drove downtown to shop. Stores that were once a big draw were experiencing a severe decline in retail business. Fewer shoppers meant fewer dollars to reinvest in the stores, and many began to look shabby and rundown. One by one, unable to combat market forces, these once popular downtown stores closed their doors across America.

As the von Maurs adjusted, they kept one thing in mind: no matter how different their stores looked or where they were located, customer service would still be priority No. 1. But the question remained. Could Petersen's preserve its reputation for understated elegance and strong customer service while launching an entirely new image for the company? They were about to find out.

Please touch the merchandise...

Six months after closing the downtown store, Petersen's opened a new store in College Square Mall in Cedar Falls, Iowa, and closed its downtown Clinton location. They were now a mall-only operation. Back at the Davenport headquarters, the Petersen's leadership team had been working for almost two years to put together a new image for their stores. But the remodel would be more than merely cosmetic; the culture within Petersen's was beginning to change. In their usual understated way, the von Maurs didn't announce their impending image makeover in the newspapers. There were no new billboards or press releases. Rather, the Duck Creek store was quietly remodeled, incorporating many of the new ideas. In the end, the transformation incorporated key features for which Von Maur is well known today. Well-lit, spacious stores; pianists and comfortable seating areas; a warmer, more enticing décor; fireplaces in some of the shoe departments; expanded women's lounges; and fresh flowers throughout. As part of this change, Petersen's eliminated entire departments, including bridal, home goods, hair salons, and furniture.

Duck Creek was the first expression of the major change. The store had a residential feel and didn't use mannequins or big signs. Instead, there were small signs that

said, "Please touch the merchandise. You'll love it." New showcases and racks were all below eye level and there were no partitions in the store. Even the support columns were mirrored so they would seem to "disappear." The carpeted selling areas were punctuated with large, upholstered chairs and couches, which also acted as upscale seating in the shoe department. Petersen's also created what many called "the nicest women's restroom lounges in the area"—ones that included couches, chairs, European-style stalls, and baby-changing rooms.

The sweeping changes caught the attention of the public and the media. An article in *Iowan* magazine in 1987 stated, "Petersen Harned Von Maur is on the move. In the last 18 months, the Davenport-based department store chain has opened a new store in a new market, launched an ambitious remodeling campaign, and boldly closed two stores. And in a dramatic and gutsy venture—almost unheard of for its brand of retailing—this family-owned company has phased out what has long been a staple of department stores: the home furnishings department. Today, except for a small gift department in each of nine retail stores, Petersen Harned Von Maur sells exclusively men's, women's, and children's fashions, plus shoes and accessories." The *Des Moines Register* published an article saying the remodel had changed the company from a popular regional retailer into an upscale, nationally recognized, department store. The positive response emboldened Petersen's to remodel all of its stores. "It was a big investment to convert our stores to this new model, particularly SouthPark in Moline, which was a fairly new store that had recently had its shoe department redone," says Jim. "I know this because I worked for the contractor who did the demolition there. I remember asking, 'You're really going to rip all of these walls out? And my dad said, 'Wait until you see it!'"

Pianos, Canaries, and Clothes

Introducing pianists to the store turned out to be one of the most-beloved aspects of the redesign. The atrium lounge area at the center of the stores features a grand piano with a pianist playing at all times the store is open. Customers were encouraged to relax on chairs and sofas and enjoy the music. The stores also reintroduced singing canaries, marking a return to a tradition started by Dick Sr. in the 1940s. "People who remember our old downtown store will recall that every January Dad would bring out the yellow canaries. It was an uplift for our customers and our people too," Dick told the *Des Moines Register.* The von Maurs featured the canaries in the stores until 2001.

Sweet Sounds

Store associates were often surprised by items unexpectedly added to their departments. As one reported, "When they told us we were getting a new addition in our cosmetics area, we thought that they meant a new fragrance. That theory was soon proven wrong when we received five male canaries. They drew a lot of attention with their beautiful singing. Unfortunately, they could not be with us forever, since they only sang in the spring. Our customers and employees enjoyed the lovely voices of our fine feathered friends, which we named Woodstock, Scooter, Herky, Buttercup, and Sir Happy."

Petersen's introduced pianos into the stores in the late 1980s. The pianos remain a central feature of the modern-day Von Maur stores.

Beyond canaries and music, Petersen's recommitted itself to offering quality products at a fair price. The company aimed its sales at a broad market, using a "good, better, best" pricing strategy that continues to this day. Petersen's had 45 buyers flying regularly to New York City, and occasionally to Chicago, Dallas, and Los Angeles, in pursuit of the latest fashions. To compete against the stronger buying power of large national competitors, the company set a goal to be "first to market" with branded apparel items. In the industry, being first to market means that in exchange for a store, such as Petersen's, taking the risk to place the first vendor order on a new fashion item, the vendor would return the favor by sending that item to the company ahead of the competition. This strategy meant Petersen's store buyers could identify bestsellers early and place large reorders before other chains had even introduced the same goods. At the same time, Petersen's tried to identify slow sellers quickly and mark them down.

Dick Sr. was an early proponent of ensuring Petersen's always had the latest fashions. He and his brothers had survived retail during World War II, an era when goods were scarce and manufacturers could not produce everything the consumer desired. Items such as automobiles, nylons, soap, and food were in limited supply. Over lunch in the downtown Tea Room, Dick Sr. often put questions to his sons and Arth. On one occasion, he asked how they would deal with a vendor selling

The newly redesigned stores featured well-lit, wide-open spaces where customers could focus on the latest fashions.

Levi's jeans. "If the vendor offered you jeans that were not selling well for half price would you buy those or would you pay full price for the newest line of jeans?" asked Dick Sr. Arth responded that he would buy a mix so he could offer both new jeans and also some that were marked down. Arth recalled that Dick Sr. said, "'Wrong. Don't do that. Go get the newest merchandise and pay full price. Bring it home and let the customer choose.' Chuck and Dick's father believed in offering the freshest fashions and letting customers decide what they did or didn't like."

But the question remained, why would a vendor give merchandise to Petersen's before some of its larger competitors, some of which bought more merchandise? Arth says part of the answer lies in the way Petersen's employees conduct themselves within the industry. "We train our buyers to always act with the highest level of integrity," Arth says. "When we buy merchandise from a vendor, we do not ask them to pay for any advertising. We don't ask for anything, and we pay full price. In exchange, we have one request. We want to

be in on the first cutting." The first cutting is an industry term that refers to when a vendor initially manufactures and launches a new, unproven, fashion design. Because Petersen's was smaller, vendors incurred less risk by providing the family-owned business with an initial cutting that would have to be much larger for a higher-volume retailer. "Being smaller definitely worked in our favor for getting fresh fashions first," Chuck says. Arth said the von Maurs' philosophy was simple: Get more of what the customers want and get rid of what they don't want.

The Cost of Doing Business

The von Maurs knew having the freshest fashions wasn't enough. They needed a highly trained sales staff on the floor to build relationships with customers. As more department store chains were cutting back on staff and centralizing their checkout counters, the von Maurs again did just the opposite. They decided to hire associates in larger numbers and reward them for efficient and friendly customer service. During this era, Arth says about 65 to 75 percent of

As more department store chains were cutting back on staff and centralizing their checkout counters, the von Maurs continued to put a priority on offering one-on-one service.

most retail sales associates in all department stores were women who worked part-time. But Petersen's wanted its associates to do more. They wanted them to know customers' names and preferences, write them thank you notes, and call them when fresh merchandise arrived. "We realized you can't do that with someone who works 15 to 20 hours a week when you are open 70 hours a week," Arth says. "We tried to go almost exclusively to full-time sales associates."

The company also made it a priority to be a family-friendly employer, not requiring associates to work major holidays when other retailers held their biggest sales. This tradition has continued. The stores are closed on New Year's Day, Easter, Memorial Day, Fourth of July, Labor Day, Thanksgiving, and Christmas. "That time is preserved for spending time with friends and family," says Dick.

Making changes in the way the company hired, trained, and rewarded associates helped Petersen's find success as it entered new markets. In 1989, the company purchased two Carson Pirie Scott stores in Illinois, one at Decatur's Hickory Point Mall and the other at Normal's College Hills Mall. They had been eyeing the College Hills location, but when Carson Pirie Scott approached them with a $4 million price tag, the brothers walked away. Carson Pirie Scott came back,

saying it would drop the price, but it would only sell if Petersen's bought both properties. They did, for $3.5 million, and opened them in July 1989.

Following the announcement of the two new stores, many anticipated Petersen's growth would slow as they entered the 1990s. "We're looking at acquisitions and new locations all the time," Chuck told *Iowan* magazine. "But neither are as plentiful as they once were, so growth is a slower process now." He went on to say that running a chain of department stores is the most competitive business in the world. "You go back in time when J.C. Penney and Sears and Wards first came to town," he said. "Independent retailers thought that was going to be the end. Then Woolworth and the other five-and-dimes and the variety stores came along, and the independents thought that was the end. Discounters and outlet malls and catalog merchandisers came along, and again there was gloom and doom. What's going on now is nothing new. It's just a bit faster, and through the use of electronic data and computers, you track things faster, move faster, and change faster. We're more excited now than we have ever been. We love the business, and we always have, but for us, the last several years have been more exciting than the first 30. There have been many changes, and we are having a lot of fun with the challenge."

For decades customers collected the company's shopping bags, which featured artwork and images from regional artists. In 2006, Von Maur changed the look of its shopping bags, which now often feature the family crest.

chapter 9

MAJOR AD-JUSTMENTS: TURNING OFF THE SPIGOT ON ADVERTISING

The von Maurs had just made big changes to their stores' interior design and now were turning their attention to a much different matter—advertising and promotion. For decades, they drew crowds to their stores with over-the-top promotions typical of department stores in that day. They brought in lions, canaries, rabbits, and reindeer. They dropped Ping-Pong® balls with coupons in the streets. And they hosted a man with a jetpack who launched himself into the sky wearing Ked's™ tennis shoes.

But Chuck and Dick were beginning to question whether the company was benefiting from all of these promotions, and particularly from newspaper advertising.

Apparently Dick Sr. had pondered the same question two decades earlier when he created a watercolor that still hangs in the corporate headquarters today. *Yesterday's News* depicts a snowy, rural landscape with a local newspaper advertisement blowing against a farmer's fence. Dick Sr. painted the scene around 1971, a year in which Petersen's spent nearly a half a million dollars on advertising. The company was not alone. Historically, department stores had been big-time advertisers. Dating back to the late 1800s, full-page advertisements in the local newspaper were commonplace. Well into the 1900s, and beyond, some of the nation's largest stores were spending nearly as much money on advertising as salaries.

Above, in 1915, J.H.C. Petersen's produced this *National Patriotic Sentimental Ragtime Songs* book for "get-acquainted gatherings, stags, luncheons, banquets, joy parties, and smokers."

Dick Sr. painted *Yesterday's News* depicting a snowy,
rural landscape with a local newspaper advertisement
blowing against a farmer's fence.

"Over the years, dating back to when our grandfather founded the company, we spent an unbelievable amount of money on advertising and marketing," says Dick. Customers who strolled past the family's Boston Store as early as 1887 were treated to elaborate store window displays, hand-painted signs touting sales, and commemorative items featuring the Boston Store name. During this era, the names Boston Store and Harned & Von Maur appeared on everything, including china plates, flour sacks, baseball bats, calendars, and more.

Ping-Pong Balls and Paperweights

The von Maurs may have learned some of their early marketing savvy from J.H.C. Petersen. Even by late 1800s standards, Petersen was ahead of his time when it came to promoting his store. On one occasion, he hung fabric over the store's exterior to promote its drapery goods. Petersen also understood that there was no better way to get customers into the store than by giving them something for free. The store gave away everything from painted blue wooden egg boxes targeted to their "farmer friends" to fabric yardsticks for ladies interested in sewing, to paperweights and jewelry boxes.

Above: By 1925, the von Maurs discovered that the mighty Mississippi River, which was just a block away, offered some unique advertising opportunities. They paid to have large banners hung on the ferry, so downtown shoppers could see them from shore.

Left: In late 1800s, fabric was hung over the store's exterior to capture the attention of customers walking by.

From Mother Goose to the Brooklyn Bridge

In 1893, the store gave away the children's book, *Jolly Jingles*, from Mother Goose. The back cover featured an advertisement for Boston Store with an inscription that read, "To our 'little' friends who, we hope, will someday be our 'big' friends as their mothers and fathers have been for years." Boston Store also published small leather books on subjects customers might find interesting, including a treatise on easy farm bookkeeping. The book had a ledger that allowed farmers to record the sale price of livestock, butter, cream, and groceries. It was also common to see expansive, full-page, illustrated newspaper ads promoting sales on items such as wool soap flakes for 9 cents or "3,000 yards of brand new summer silk: 75 cent, 85 cent, and $1 grades, 49 cents/yd." But it was the von Maur's window displays that often garnered the most attention.

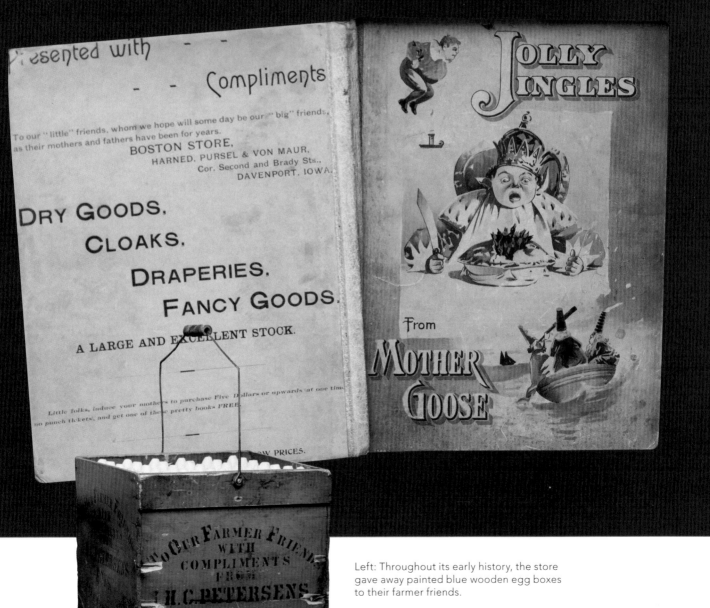

Left: Throughout its early history, the store gave away painted blue wooden egg boxes to their farmer friends.

In 1891, hoping to draw customers away from rival
J.H.C. Petersen & Sons, Boston Store unveiled a
window display of 10,000 spools of Brooks Cotton that
were used to create a replica of the Brooklyn Bridge.

During the 1950s, Petersen's store windows were becoming more and more sophisticated.

After Harned & Von Maur and Petersen's merged to become one store in 1928, the new Petersen Harned Von Maur spent even more on marketing. Over the next six decades, few expenses were spared. During one event, Chuck and Dick dropped Ping-Pong balls from the downtown store's rooftop onto a waiting crowd. As the balls bounced everywhere, including under cars and into gutters, eager customers collected them. Some of the balls contained coupons and gift certificates related to the sale. "It was absolutely crazy, and a lot of fun," Chuck remembers with a laugh. "I don't think the city was too happy with us though, because it caused quite a traffic jam. The downside was that women who had ripped her hose crawling on the ground after the balls then came into the store and demanded new hosiery. That was something we hadn't expected, but we certainly obliged."

During this period, Petersen's store windows were becoming more sophisticated. In addition to showing merchandise, they offered commentary on the day's news and events. It was a full-time job keeping them up to date.

A Sale for Every Occasion

For years, Petersen's biggest and most popular store sales were Ladies Day, Founder's Day, Anniversary Day, George Washington's Birthday, Customer Appreciation Day, Sidewalk Sales, pre-Christmas, Christmas, and after the holidays. They also held "Private Letter" Sales. On one occasion a printing error led to the most successful Downtown Night Sale on record. The event had been scheduled for a Wednesday, but misprinted invitations brought shoppers to the store on Saturday. *The Petersen Post* reported, "The figures showed Saturday was by far the better night to have the sale, in comparison to previous night sales during the work week! The store was absolutely packed with customers in every department."

Left: During one event, Petersen's dropped Ping-Pong balls from the downtown store's rooftop onto a waiting crowd.

Above: Petersen's annual bridal and fashion shows drew large crowds.

The company's women's apparel departments also hosted style shows with models changing their clothes every few minutes and strolling through every department. Spring fashion shows were also a hit. In April 1980, the show theme was "Clothes for the Petersen Family" and it featured 17 models wearing items such as "pants," "soft suits," "How the West Was Worn," and "Romance of Spring." Over the decades, Petersen's ran page after page of advertisements. The von Maurs often joked that they might as well have owned the local newspaper since they spent so much money on advertising. On weekends, Petersen's was known to run sale ads 40 pages long.

Pole Benders, Lions, and JetPacks

When Chuck and Dick entered the business in the 1950s, they brought their own style of marketing. During one celebration, they hired a pole-bending circus act. The performer climbed a pole perched on the store's roof, repeatedly riding the arced pole down to the roofline and back up into the air. "When we opened that day there were only three people on the street," Dick recalls with a laugh. "It was a flop with the general public, but our employees really enjoyed it." Another promotion drew much larger

crowds. In the mid-1960s, a man playing the role of Kolonel Keds arrived at Petersen's downtown store with his jetpack. He was part of a nationwide tour to promote Keds® new line of athletic shoes. Bell Aerosystems had only recently developed the jetpack, and Keds used the eye-popping technology to draw crowds wherever it went. Outside the store, Kolonel Keds laced up his new shoes, slung a jetpack on his back, and took off in the air, rising four to five stories before returning to the street to great applause.

The von Maurs remember one Easter display that went a bit too far. The first day it featured two rabbits, but soon the local J.C. Penney store manager called Dick Sr. to tell him he had noticed that two had multiplied to six. Chuck and Dick decided, "That was the end of that display!"

Above: Kolonel Keds and his jetpack visited Petersen's during a national marketing promotion aimed at promoting athletic shoes.

Celebrities Stop By

On one occasion Tom Mix, an American film actor who starred in early Western movies between 1910 and 1935, appeared at the store with his horse and drew large crowds of admiring fans. Other special guests included Roy Rogers' horse, Trigger, and Emmet Kelly, an American circus performer who created the memorable clown figure "Weary Willie." Over the years, many celebrities came to shop. Actor Robert Young of the television series *Dr. Marcus Welby*, Jon Hager of the Hager twins who appeared on *Hee Haw*, and Red Skelton all visited Petersen's stores.

During one celebration, Petersen's hired a pole-bending circus act. The performer climbed a pole perched on the store's roof, repeatedly riding the arced pole down to the roofline and back up into the air.

In the 1950s, Petersen's downtown store added a new feature at the holidays—a neon sign that ran the full length of the building and featured leaping reindeer and a holiday message for customers.

One Scoop or Two?

Occasionally, new ideas went a step too far. In the 1970s, Petersen's set up an old-fashioned ice cream fountain in the downtown Davenport store's front window. Customers waited in line to eat ice cream at tables in the store's window displays. But that ended quickly when a city health inspector said the store was violating the city code because there was not direct access to running water. "We had to shut the whole thing down, but it was a lot of fun while it lasted," Chuck says.

During one promotion, Petersen's cleared out the store's toy department to make room for a caged lion and tiger. "It stank to high heaven," the brothers said, "but it really drew a crowd."

H. VON MAUR'S LONG FLIGHT IN AIRPLANE

Up About an Hour and Dropped Hundreds of Tags on City.

Henry Von Maur, of the firm of Harned & Von Maur, is now an aviation booster, after a ride of about an hour in one of Frank Wallace's planes Saturday morning. They left Wallace Field and flew around north and west of the city till they gained an altitude of several thousand feet, after which they came over the city, Mr. Von Maur throwing out about three-fourths of a large supply of prize tags which they had taken up with them. The remainder, after the trip, were tossed from the roof of the Harned & Von Maur store after the return to town.

"It was a wonderful experience," declared Mr. Von Maur after the flight. "I intend to go up again as soon as I can. Mr. Wallace surprised me after our return by saying that one little "dip" he made with the plane was a drop of 1,400 feet. I didn't know it, and thought it just an ordinary bit of rather steep descent."

Please DO NOT CLIMB ON RAILING   Please DO NOT CLIMB ON RAILING

Christmas Eve in t   Enchanted Forest

Christmas at Petersen's

Through it all, Petersen's reserved its biggest and most impressive marketing efforts for the Christmas holiday, a cherished tradition within the store. Customers came from near and far to see the downtown store's beautiful window displays. David Heitz wrote in 2006 about his memory of the Petersen's window displays. "I hate to admit it, but I lost that magical Christmas spirit many years ago. Last Saturday, I found it again. A trip to the [Bettendorf] Family Museum was all it took to flip my switch and get me humming *Deck the Halls*. The second I saw the mechanical 'Santa's Workshop' display, it took me back 30 years to when I was six years old." For years, the display—which features elves chopping wood and making toys while Santa sits in a chair, his belly jiggling with each "Ho, ho, ho"—delighted children and adults who marveled at the setup through the big, storefront windows at Petersen's.

One year, Petersen's transformed a portion of the store basement, adjacent to the popular Tea Room, into a "Magical Christmas Wonderland." The idea was to attract more people to the Tea Room and celebrate the holidays. Moments before the "Enchanted Birch Trees" attraction opened, the fire department shut it down, saying the combination of sapling trees and twinkling lights was a fire hazard. Another year, Petersen's brought in live reindeer, which had to be removed because they were creating too big a mess. But one thing remained constant over the years: the long lines of children waiting to see Santa and listen to carolers. The von Maurs are still nostalgic about the days of special events.

By the mid-1980s, Petersen's leadership team began to notice that department store chains nationwide were becoming more

Each year, Petersen's new window displays were kept covered until they could be unveiled during the annual Thanksgiving parade. Some Christmas window displays were so popular the von Maurs had to erect barriers to keep people from pushing on the glass.

aggressive with their marketing efforts, often inflating the price of regular merchandise and then having a "sale" that brought it back down to its regular price. "We didn't think it was fair to the customers," Chuck says. "We wanted to price our merchandise at a fair price. Advertising was really for sale goods, and that is not what we were about. We kept wondering why we were spending so much money promoting marked down goods and so little money on working to have the best fashion available in our stores at a fair price." The cost of advertising didn't end with paying for newspaper space. It impacted productivity and the bottom line. Petersen's buyers spent hours, and sometimes days, searching for items to feature in weekly ads. This meant they had less time to find new merchandise. The company also employed half a dozen people in its advertising

department who worked full-time on placing ads in newspapers and on television throughout Iowa and Illinois.

Now that the company had stopped selling home goods, the brothers felt they needed to change their advertising strategy. "When our store was in the business of selling home goods, we felt like we had to advertise them," Arth says, "because we knew that people rarely woke up in the morning with a burning desire to go buy a new appliance. If we wanted them to buy their home goods at our store, we had to promote them. On the other hand, we believed that with fashion, people would come to the store on their own to see the latest styles."

It was time to test this theory. The von Maurs wanted to see what would happen if they

The von Maurs drove this car to
promote the store in local parades.

...are getting ready for Christmas!

All too soon it was nightime. The whole family gathered around the organ to sing carols —everybody but Judy, that is...

'Pears as though a cow would have some natural advantages in gift wrapping.

Through it all, Petersen's reserved its biggest and most impressive marketing efforts for the Christmas holiday, a cherished tradition within the store.

phased out advertising, which consumed about 4 percent of their sales dollars. They suspected many customers would continue to shop at their stores even if they didn't advertise in the local newspapers. "This was a gradual thing," explains Arth. "It wasn't a sudden decision, and we didn't do it all at once." The more the von Maurs thought about the concept behind advertising, the more they felt it went against their core mission of serving customers. "We believed our customers would come back on their own if we gave them fresh fashions that were well made and fairly priced," Arth says. "If you have fresh merchandise, and you get it before everyone else, then you don't need an ad to sell it."

By 1991, Von Maur had turned off the spigot on advertising. Most department stores spend between 3 to 4 percent of their annual sales on advertising. As of 2014, Von Maur was spending less than 1 percent on advertising and social media and running only a few cosmetic ads or back-to-school inserts created in partnership with its vendors. When it opens a new store, the company does some introductory advertising, but, as far as the von Maurs know, they run the only department store in the nation that uses little to no advertising. Their philosophy is to redirect the money the company saves on advertising back into customer service

benefits, such as no-interest credit card accounts, free shipping, and gift wrapping. "The best thing we can do is treat a customer well, and they'll tell their friends," Arth told the *Lombard Daily Herald* in 1994.

When others in the industry heard the von Maurs had done away with advertising, many thought it was a disastrous misstep. Arth recalls overhearing a woman at a symphony performance say she thought the company would never survive. "She said it just didn't make sense to her," Arth says with a laugh. "Then she told me she was the publisher of the newspaper. Right then, I knew I shouldn't bother saying another word!"

"Spring's on the Wing" at Petersen's

ROTHMOOR

Suits at a New LOWER Price $59.95

❖ Crisp, long-wearing worsteds! Beautiful suede cloths! Imported tweeds!

❖ Beautiful shades of engine red! Ticket green! Butter yellow! Heather pink! Navy!

❖ Styles for the college and career girl . . . for the woman with the more mature figure and for you, who are 5'4" and under.

❖ So much style for this low 1950 price!

Suit Shop — Third Floor

Petersen Harned Von Maur
DAVENPORT — IOWA

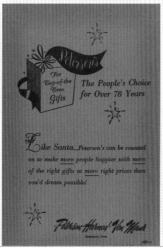

Petersen's advertised for years on the back
of community playbills.

(Photos courtesy of the German American
Heritage Center)

chapter 10

OUR ENDURING PHILOSOPHY: TREAT CUSTOMERS LIKE FAMILY

By the early 1990s, the von Maurs had eliminated home goods and most of its advertising and established the company as the only family-owned department store chain in the United States, offering a unique combination of well-appointed stores, interest-free credit, free gift wrapping, and free shipping nationwide. "The company's goal is to tend to shoppers' every need, wish, or desire from the time they enter the store to the time they leave," wrote a *Yorktown Daily Herald* reporter in a 1994 article. "In fact, sales associates are trained to take care of shoppers' needs even long after that shopper has left the store."

Many in the industry believe one of the reasons the company survived the Great Depression, the development of suburban malls, and the age of conglomerates and corporate takeovers is because it consistently maintained a high standard of customer service. Store founder C.J. von Maur once famously said, "Treat every customer like family; commit to quality and service; Rule No. 1 is the customer is always right; and Rule No. 2 is if you think the customer is wrong, refer back to Rule No. 1." More than 140 years later, the employee handbook still reflects C.J.'s thoughts. Among them: "Never argue with a customer. Listen to their complaints, and treat them with the greatest respect as you would like to be treated."

Above: In the early 2000s, a customer returned a dress that had been purchased in the 1950s and still had the original tags with the store name Harned & Von Maur.

Don Daily, a longtime shoe
salesman at Petersen's, helps a
woman try on a new pair of shoes.

For generations, store associates have lived by the creed that every transaction deserves their best attention, regardless of whether it is a large or small purchase or a return. The last sale of the day, the handbook states, must be handled as courteously as the first. "Customers are guests in our store and expect friendly and knowledgeable service," the handbook continues. "We expect our employees to live up to our customers' expectations, discontinuing stock work, conversations, or other business to assist our customers. Know your merchandise so that you are able to select items that appeal to each customer. Cooperation is important. We expect it from you, and you can depend on it from us. Consideration and cooperation between co-workers establishes a pleasant atmosphere and enables us to serve customers more effectively."

Dick Sr. filled a leather-bound journal with ideas he thought were relevant to the company's values. Next to a log of company sales in the book was a poem called, "Good Business." Thought to be originally written by Edgar A. Guest. In part, it reads:

If I possessed a shop or store
I'd drive the grouches off my floor.
I'd never let some gloomy guy
Offend the folks who come to buy.
I'd never keep the boy or clerk
With a mental toothache at his work.
Nor let a man who draws his pay
Drive a customer of ours away.
I'd treat the man who takes our time, and spends
a nickel or a dime,
with courtesy and make him feel that I was
pleased to close the deal.
Because tomorrow who can tell
He may want the goods I have to sell
And in that case then glad he'll be
To spend his dollars all with me.
The reason people pass one door
To patronize another store
Is not necessarily because the busier place
Has better silks, or gloves, or lace.
Or cheaper prices but it likely lies
In pleasant words or smiling eyes.
The only difference, I believe,
Is in the treatment folks receive.

Von Maur associates are still known for sending handwritten notes to customer's homes thanking them for visiting the store and inviting them to come back soon. Most sales associates know many of their customer's names by heart, something almost unheard of in today's retail world. Elizabeth Orman told *Crain's Chicago Business* that she shops at the St. Charles Von Maur store regularly because of the service. "If they don't have what you're looking for, they will do their best to find it at another store and send it to the house," Orman says.

Since the early days of operating a large, downtown department store, the von Maurs have understood the value of having knowledgeable and accessible associates on the floor. When a new store opens, the company often brings in sales associates from its well-established stores to work alongside the new staff, ensuring that customers receive excellent service from day one. "When I visited the competition, it was becoming clear that our stores were better organized, brighter, and cleaner," says Jim, who is now the company president. "But what I also noticed is that while other stores had one sales person in a department, we had three or four. It made a big difference for our customers. I remember thinking that I was so glad to be part of an organization that was striving to do something better."

The von Maurs still have the original stepping stone employees and customers used to climb into carriages.

Through the years, the store adopted many different modes of delivery. In the late 1800s, a store horse and buggy brought goods to customers' homes. By the early 1900s, Harned & Von Maur introduced same-day delivery for in-town customers, using a new "fleet" of three delivery trucks. In the mid-1970s, the company stopped using its own trucks and contracted with a commercial service, allowing the retailer to expand its customer base and deliver packages across the nation. In 2015, between stores and ecommerce, Von Maur shipped 776,485 packages.

It's a Wrap

Another more obvious display of the company's customer service philosophy is reflected in the way associates dress. The independent store chain is known for its professional dress code. Female associates wear dresses or skirts. Men wear a coat and tie. The handbook says, "All employees represent the company to the public, regardless of their job function. Therefore, it is necessary to project a neat and professional image. While changes in fashion may generally seem acceptable, they may not always be professional."

By far, the customer service benefits shoppers say they enjoy most are the interest-free credit card, free gift wrapping with any purchase, and free delivery anywhere in the United States. If a customer purchases too much to carry home, or wants to ship the gift to a relative or friend across the country, they can do that in the store at no extra cost. "I think we are one of the few retailers in the country that offers that kind of service," Jim says. "And as the cost of the U.S. Postal Service and other delivery systems continue to rise, this has become a big incentive for customers to shop with us."

In 2015, Von Maur used approximately 4,600 rolls (721 miles) of gift wrap and nearly 16,950 rolls (935 miles) of ribbon.

Shoppers regularly tell associates they buy Von Maur Christmas presents so they can put the beautifully wrapped packages under their trees. Other stores have tried to offer free gift wrapping and shipping, but never continued the services for very long. "It's harder for public companies to take these steps," Jim says. "This is where being a small and agile company is an advantage in the marketplace." Arth agrees, saying interest-free credit, free shipping, and free gift wrapping have helped the company move into larger markets and compete successfully. "People were always asking, 'how do you compete?'" Arth says. "I told them there are a lot of ways, but you have to think like a customer. You have to look past profits and losses. If customers like what you are doing, they will come back."

Arth says he is proud the company is one of the few that has been able to build its customer service philosophy into its design. Well-lit stores, comfortable sofas, pianists playing live music, and spacious women's lounges all contribute to an atmosphere that makes shoppers feel welcome. "It all came together," Arth says. "When we saw what we had created, it gave us all great confidence. We thought we could go into larger cities and do well against some of the nation's largest stores. Some people were talking about how this little company from Iowa could compete amongst the giants and get the customer to shop there, even without advertising."

When the Hickory Point store was recruiting at a local college fair, a professor of marketing stopped by the Von Maur booth to tell associates how pleased he and his wife were with the store's customer service. He proceeded to explain that each semester when his class discusses customer service and how it relates to marketing, he uses the Von Maur store as a shining example.

"I Want to Compliment You..."

Associates are known for going the extra mile to help customers.

One customer sent a glowing letter to Petersen's in fall 1979. At the time, Petersen's was located just a few blocks from the Mississippi River, which meant they often attracted people vacationing in the area. The letter stated, "My sister and I were in your store for a short time on a recent trip aboard the Mississippi Queen. I just want to tell you we did not find a store as nice as yours anywhere along our excursion. We had shopped in Minneapolis, Indianapolis, St. Louis, and Columbus. We were very impressed with your store."

Even in the early days, Petersen's associates alerted customers that new merchandise had arrived. "Mrs. Munro, we have our Toastmaster oven broilers in, and I have saved one for you. Housewares Department, Marjorie Dawson. PHVM."

chapter 11

GOODBYE PETERSEN'S.
HELLO VON MAUR.

As the 1990s drew near, Petersen's became the largest fashion department store group in Iowa, and after 117 years, it simplified its corporate name from Petersen Harned Von Maur to Von Maur. Neither Harned nor Petersen had been associated with the department stores for more than 50 years, and keeping their names only confused customers who would ask where the two men were. The von Maurs often joked among themselves, "Petersen is dead. Harned isn't feeling so well, and the von Maurs are still at it!" Since 1872, the company had been known by many different names: J.H.C. Petersen & Sons; Harned, Pursel & Von Maur; Boston Store; Harned, Bergner & Von Maur, Harned & Von Maur, Harned & Von Maur/J.H.C. Petersen & Sons (two stores, one owner) and Petersen Harned Von Maur (aka Petersen's or Pete's). For the first time, it would bear only the Von Maur name.

Shortly before the name change, Jack Arth became the first person outside the von Maur family to be named president. So, ironically, instead of a member of the family, it was Arth who announced the new name on April 21, 1989, "This is a natural simplification of the three-word name. Von Maur expresses what we are today—a fashion store that places customer service first."

Nine months later, Von Maur moved its offices and distribution center from the

Hangers have always created a lot of work for Von Maur associates. Often they become bent or tangled and have to be hand-sorted before they are shipped back to headquarters to be reused. In 2016, Von Maur used more than 8 million hangers.

The company expands beyond Iowa and Illinois
with a new store in Omaha, Nebraska, circa 1995.

downtown Davenport store building to new corporate headquarters in a vacated outlet mall on the outskirts of the city. The company remodeled the space to match its store décor. The headquarters featured ponds, trees, and green space around the building, creating a park-like atmosphere. The new location, just blocks from Interstate 80, allowed Von Maur to streamline its distribution process. Having the headquarters on one level made it more efficient to move merchandise, and a state-of-the-art trolley system processed merchandise on hangers faster. Better and faster distribution was becoming more and more important as Von Maur's annual sales continued to grow.

By the 1990s, Von Maur had its sights set on entering the highly competitive Chicago market. Some in the industry questioned whether the Iowa-based retailer could survive in a place characterized more by rooftops than cornfields. Chicago was only three hours from the corporate headquarters, but it was worlds apart when it came to competition. The company would be up against stores that had dominated the Chicago retail market for decades. And, for the first time, it would compete with larger, national stores, some of which were only now entering the Chicago market as well.

Above: The stone nameplate etching from the company's original building was proudly installed at corporate headquarter in 2015.

Right: In 1999, Von Maur featured Quad City artist John Holladay's colorful map that captured the company's growth over the years.

Some retail analysts speculated that Von Maur would have to change its company philosophy and start advertising and holding weekly sales. Many Chicago shoppers had been lifelong Marshall Field's, Neiman Marcus, Lord & Taylor, Carson Pirie Scott, and Saks Fifth Avenue customers. Nearly all of these national chains spent millions of dollars advertising in the *Chicago Sun Times* and *Chicago Tribune.* Combined, these newspapers had the ability to reach more than a million customers each week. But the von Maurs believed the company's ability to offer the best customer service and fresh fashions would spread by word of mouth. "The truth is that we didn't really think we could have afforded to advertise in the Chicago newspapers even if we had wanted to," Chuck says with a laugh.

The opportunity to move into the Chicago market emerged in 1993. The von Maurs visited a Yorktown mall anchor store space in Lombard, Illinois, in the western suburbs. A retail friend had tipped them off that the J.C. Penney and Carson Pirie Scott stores there had been among those company's top stores. Chuck and Dick could sense an opportunity, but there were a few significant problems. Yorktown had not been remodeled in decades. Newer, more attractive malls were popping up and drawing customers away. The mall's decline had begun in 1987 when

Wieboldt's, a once popular Chicago-based discount retailer, declared bankruptcy and closed its Yorktown store. For seven years, the cavernous and out-of-date store stood empty, becoming an eyesore and serving as a constant reminder to shoppers that the mall was no longer thriving. While other stores shied away from the neglected space, Von Maur saw possibilities. The space would have to be completely renovated anyway. The company entered negotiations with Pehrson-Long Associates, hoping to purchase the space at a good price, but negotiations stalled for nearly three years. Needing to give new life to the deal, the mall owners approached Lombard village officials about providing financial incentives to make the deal happen. The officials responded with a now familiar refrain, "What's Von Maur?" The brothers had faced this name recognition problem for decades, and it didn't deter them. After introducing Lombard officials to their stores,

Company headquarters relocated on Feb. 19, 1990, from the former Petersen's downtown Davenport store to a location on the north side of Davenport near Interstate 80.

On July 18, 1994, Von Maur opened at Yorktown Center in Lombard, Illinois, creating its largest store at the time.

the village was eager to rebate some of the company's annual sales tax receipts. Yorktown also announced it would undergo a multi-million mall remodeling program. On July 18, 1994, Von Maur opened at Yorktown Center, creating its largest store to date. When the renovation was complete, all that remained of the Wieboldt's store was its four exterior walls. Once again, the company had seen potential where others saw decay.

Instead of advertising in the Chicago newspapers to announce its presence, Von Maur sent brochures to nearby residents announcing the grand opening and highlighting the company's history and unique interest-free charge cards. But after the initial opening, sales struggled. Looking back, the management team can cite a number of reasons. First, Yorktown's mall remodel was still under way and hadn't resulted in increased customer traffic. Second, and perhaps most important, the company dramatically miscalculated the store's first-year sales. The store's inventory had been based on the number of shoppers who lived within a five-mile radius of the mall. "We looked at the volume we were doing in West Des Moines and thought we needed at least twice the merchandise, but that was way off," Arth says. Dick agrees and recalls, "Another one of our great mistakes."

It was during this time that Ric von Maur, Dick's older son, held several positions at

Valley West, NorthPark, and Muscatine stores before running the Yorktown store at the young age of 27. He was the first of the fourth generation to join the family business. From his first day at Yorktown, Ric and his associates had a new challenge. Urban shoppers refused to believe there was such a thing as interest-free charge cards. "Ric opened the store, and he would tell customers about our free-interest card, and they would say… 'What's the catch?'" his younger brother, Jim, recalls. "They would read the fine print and say 'aha' and act like there was a catch. My brother would tell them there is no catch. They were convinced we were making it up." Even when Ric explained that more than 60 percent of all Von Maur customers were using the interest-free charge cards at their 11 stores, it had little effect. Customers simply thought it was too good to be true.

The store also was turning merchandise slower than expected. "Honestly, it was an abysmal start," Jim says. "We couldn't find a place to store all of the merchandise. We had to cancel the orders for some and find a new home for others. We also had to mark down goods." As a result, 1994 would go down as the least profitable year in the company's history. "We were the new kid on the block, no one knew about us, and we ran no ads," Jim says. Other retailers were struggling as well. Von Maur needed to take a hard look at its new store and turn things around. Closing it was not an option. "The good news was that Valley West in Des Moines bailed us out by taking excess merchandise and selling it," says Arth. Despite the slow start, word of mouth took over before the end of the first year. Customers' lauded key features in the new store, including its extensive shoe selection, elaborate gift-wrap station, men's shoe-shine area, and marble flooring throughout the store. After the first year, sales for the entire mall had jumped more than 20 percent; many credited Von Maur. "There is not a mall in Chicago that is having the increases Yorktown is having," Robert Long, president of Pehrson-Long Associates, was quoted as saying. Arth was pleased with the success. "Once customers began to trust our formula of no interest, great merchandise, free gift wrapping, and free shipping, we started to take off," he says. In the coming years, the Yorktown store became Von Maur's largest volume store.

Jim Joins the Business

As Von Maur entered Chicago, Ric's younger brother, Jim, joined the family business. When Jim graduated from college in 1992, his father, Dick, suggested he work for another store before deciding whether he wanted to pursue a career in retail. Jim spent a year working for two competitors in the greater Chicago market. That experience, he says, helped shape his career path and his retail philosophy. Among other things, he walked away convinced that operating the family stores on a strictly commission-based sales model created a poor shopping environment. That model often caused associates to compete for customers (sometimes even hiding merchandise from one another, so they could sell the best and highest-priced goods), something Jim did not want to see happen at Von Maur. Jim took that perspective with him when he entered Von Maur's executive training program in 1993. "It was interesting, and I think I started to see the future," he says. "We weren't going to be just some downtown store and stagnant. I could see we were growing and had momentum, and we had motivated people working for us. All of that piqued my interest."

During his time in the executive training program, Jim sold shoes and sportswear, became a department manager and buyer, and acted as personnel manager at the SouthPark store. He also watched his father and uncle make tough choices about the future. As Von Maur moved into larger markets, the company had to evaluate its smaller stores. As a result, on Dec. 24, 1994, Von Maur closed its Muscatine Mall location, which had been open for 15 years. "Even though I was just entering the business, I knew that going into Chicago took a lot of moxie by my father and my uncle," Jim says. "It was a huge investment and the fact that it ended up working out said to us that the formula does not just work in Iowa and Illinois. It works in big metro areas. Now, America is your oyster."

Jim von Maur   Ric von Maur

The Next Generation

Jim von Maur started in the Von Maur's executive
training program in 1993 after some time working for
competitors in the greater Chicago market.

It was during this time that Ric von Maur, Dick's
older son, worked in merchandising. He would go on
to help open and manage the company's new Yorktown
store at the young age of 27.

Welcome to Nebraska

It was the mid-1990s, and Chuck's daughter, Allison, joined the family business and became part of a team tasked with opening the first Von Maur outside Iowa and Illinois. On Aug. 5, 1995, the new, three-level store at Westroads Shopping Center in Omaha opened. Von Maur was the first new retail anchor to be added to an Omaha mall since Dillard's opened in 1988. The company applied lessons learned in Chicago to make the Omaha opening a success, including stocking more than 100,000 shoes. "We didn't over-merchandise this one," Arth says with a laugh. "This store was about 50 percent larger than our West Des Moines store, so we knew what we were dealing with." Jim took over as store manager after the first year. "When I came on board, I remember thinking, 'This is the most impressive store I have ever seen.' Sales started to greatly improve after that first year."

With the Chicago and Omaha stores now established, Von Maur had 12 stores in three states generating sales that exceeded national retail averages. The retailer now had its eye on growing the business throughout the Midwest.

Left: The Von Maur management team for the new Omaha store, from left: Dave Burke, director of operations; Mike Schneider, Omaha store manager; Nancy DeDoncker, director of stores; and far right, Chuck's daughter, Allison, who managed store personnel issues and was a floor manager at the store for two years. In 1997, she left the family business to pursue other interests.

Omaha Store Hit by Tragedy in 2007

Von Maur employees, their friends, and families experienced the hardest day in the company's history on Dec. 5, 2007, when an assailant entered their store in Omaha, Nebraska, and randomly shot at customers and employees. Eight people were killed and five others were injured. Victims included customers Gary Scharf and John McDonald and employees Angie Schuster, Maggie Webb, Janet Jorgensen, Diane Trent, Gary Joy, and Beverly Flynn. Injured in the shooting were Fred Wilson, Mickey Oldham, Jeff Schaffart, and Mandy Hyda. The von Maur family says the event "was the most tragic point and time in the company's history."

Above: Jim von Maur, left, president of Von Maur department stores, stands at a makeshift memorial outside the Omaha department store with his parents, Dick and Sue von Maur.

(AP Photo/Eric Francis)

chapter 12

FASHIONING SUCCESS

Few could have foreseen that in the next 15 years Von Maur would expand into larger markets, such as Atlanta and New York, and become one of the last independent, family-owned-and-operated department stores in the United States. By the end of the 1980s, the retail scene across the country had dramatically changed. The era of store mergers and acquisitions was in full swing. Stores were bought and sold and changed names almost as fast as they changed merchandise.

As one writer in *Footwear News* noted in 1995, "It's doubtful whether R.H. Macy, Abraham Abraham, Lazarus Straus, Morris Rich, Simon Lazarus, William Filene, Lyman Bloomingdale, Eben Jordan or Benjamin Marsh could ever have imagined the dry

goods emporiums they founded and nurtured would one day be part of one giant $14 billion department store conglomerate. But Federated Department Stores—and to a lesser degree, May Department Stores Co. with sales of $9.8 billion—have, over the course of the past decade, amassed a collection of stellar retail nameplates and combined them into power-houses with buying clout unprecedented."

Many independent stores simply could not compete against the larger conglomerates, and they elected to sell their stores or close their doors. According to *Service and Style*, more than 360 known independent stores had closed their doors as of 2014. Some sooner than others. Chicago's hometown retail

In 2013, Von Maur moved its Iowa City store a few miles away to Iowa River Landing in Coralville, Iowa.

pioneer Marshall Field sold its family-owned department store in the 1980s, setting off a flurry of ownership changes that spanned two decades. The retail industry was becoming more complicated than ever before. During this era, the von Maur family had a few opportunities to sell, but they rebuffed the offers. In the mid-1990s, Profitt's Inc. (later Saks Inc.) approached Von Maur when it was buying other regional department stores, including Carson Pirie Scott. But the von Maurs knew that as long as members of the family were interested in running the business, they believed it would remain a privately held company.

During this time, the company underwent a number of management changes. Arth became president, Ric was named vice president of

merchandise, and Jim moved from personnel manager in Moline to the Omaha store. Ric and Jim were becoming a growing part of the executive management team and, in just a few years, would take over leadership of the family business.

It was against this backdrop in 1997 that Von Maur generated record sales. Unfortunately, its success also made the company a target of larger, national department store chains, which saw Von Maur as a growing threat. By the spring of 1997, these retailers began to flex their muscles by working to keep Von Maur out of new and existing malls throughout the nation. The first sign of trouble came when Ric and Jim attended an annual real estate convention in Las Vegas. They planned to meet with some of the

On Aug. 3, 2002, Von Maur opened Towne East Square in Wichita, Kansas.

nation's largest developers to find out about future mall openings, but they were making little headway. "Finally, the developers at the convention came right out and told us, 'We are not doing any new malls with Von Maur,'" Jim recalls. "Ric and I couldn't figure out what was going on. We were hearing the same thing over and over, and we were worried."

Baffled, the brothers approached a longtime business associate who told them some major retailers had approached developers saying they would not commit to any new mall projects if Von Maur was offered a space. "When we heard this, it made our hearts sink," Jim says. "We thought we would never be able to open a new store again. In some cases, retailers wouldn't let us in. In other cases, developers would tell us they wanted Lord & Taylor instead of Von Maur. The irony is that over the years Lord & Taylor was not successful in the Midwest, and later started to vacate some of its locations. Now many of those malls would love to have us."

Von Maur faced an uphill battle. Because it was a smaller company, it had to be willing to do things a little differently. The opportunity to take a new path arrived in October 1997 when Montgomery Ward, operating under Chapter 11 protection, announced it would close 48 stores. Over the next three years

Montgomery Ward continued to decline, and by 2000 it went out of business, closing another 227 stores. Von Maur decided to look at spaces Wards was vacating. "This is something we may not have even considered if we hadn't encountered problems at the Las Vegas convention," Jim says. In 1998, Von Maur purchased two former Ward stores in Indianapolis at Castleton Square Mall and Greenwood Park Mall. Arth, who was about to retire after a decade as president, says it was clear the company needed a new strategy for growth as it transitioned to a new leadership team. Ric would soon become president and concentrate on merchandise, and Jim would be named vice president and focus on store operations.

"These experiences had a tremendous influence on the two young men coming into the new business," Arth says. "They had to think…How are we going to do this? It would be awesome in their minds to figure out how to get some new locations. Ric and Jim knew they were going to have to try some new things. Fortunately, Chuck and Dick had shown all of us over the years how to do things differently. We had to compete or lose."

On Sept. 26, 1998, Von Maur opened at Castleton Square Mall in Indianapolis.

Loyal Customers

Von Maur has incredibly loyal customers, and there is no better example than Rosanne Pawlik (pictured right) from Glenview, Illinois. She set a goal of visiting every Von Maur store in the nation. As of 2016, she had visited 24 locations, shopping and taking photos with store managers along the way.

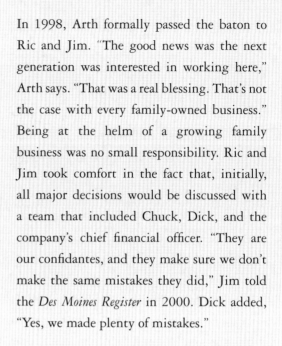

In 1998, Arth formally passed the baton to Ric and Jim. "The good news was the next generation was interested in working here," Arth says. "That was a real blessing. That's not the case with every family-owned business." Being at the helm of a growing family business was no small responsibility. Ric and Jim took comfort in the fact that, initially, all major decisions would be discussed with a team that included Chuck, Dick, and the company's chief financial officer. "They are our confidantes, and they make sure we don't make the same mistakes they did," Jim told the *Des Moines Register* in 2000. Dick added, "Yes, we made plenty of mistakes."

A New Market Entry Point: Lifestyle Centers

As the new management team pondered the future, "lifestyle centers" were popping up around the country. Instead of operating as enclosed malls, lifestyle centers combined the traditional retail functions of a shopping mall with leisure activities and amenities, such as movie theaters, coffee shops, condominiums, upscale grocery stores, and plenty of parking. These centers, often located in suburban areas, had been around since the 1980s, but they really took off over the next two decades. From 2000 to 2002, the number of lifestyle centers in the nation grew from 30 to 120. During

On Aug. 7, 1999, Von Maur opened its
first lifestyle center store in the new
SouthPointe Pavilions in Lincoln, Nebraska.

Flying High

Von Maur prides itself on giving each of its stores a special, local touch. For example, Glenview, Illinois, had been the home of an important WWII Naval Air Station. The von Maurs hung an N2S Stearman aircraft in the atrium above the escalators and installed an animated figure called Smitty, a life-like, coin-operated storyteller who shares the history of Glenview Naval Air Station.

that period, a growing number of traditional shopping malls were shutting down. From a business perspective, lifestyle centers offered a number of advantages over malls: they required less land and provided a different shopping experience. The centers appeared to offer new hope for small and large retailers who wanted to enter markets dominated by traditional, enclosed shopping centers.

"Lifestyle centers opened up a whole new opportunity for us," Jim says. "They gave us a solution to our biggest challenge: how we were going to expand into new markets. We aren't like some stores who just buy land and then throw up a building." On Aug. 7, 1999, as company-wide sales continued to increase, Von Maur opened its first lifestyle center store in the new SouthPointe Pavilions in Lincoln, Nebraska. A month later, it closed its Duck Creek location, which had been the company's first mall store 27 years earlier. The closing was the beginning of a shift in the company's business strategy, moving away from smaller towns and into larger markets.

"We had anticipated there was a strong possibility it would close, given its evolution into one of the top department stores in the country," said Dave Smith, the president of mall owner Equity Growth Group. "The industry has changed, and it has evolved into one of the top two or three department stores in the country..."

By 2000, Von Maur was growing in every way possible. It had expanded its corporate headquarters in Davenport and grown to nearly 3,000 employees. In 2001, Ric stepped down as president from the family business, and Jim assumed the top position at just 31 years of age. Dick and Chuck remained as co-chairmen. As the new century dawned, Von Maur strengthened its position in the Midwest, opening new stores in Eden Prairie Center, a Minneapolis suburb; Jefferson Pointe in Fort Wayne, Indiana; and Charlestowne Mall in St. Charles, Illinois.

While other retailers lost ground after the Sept. 11, 2001, terrorist attacks and subsequent downturn in the economy, Von Maur continued to expand. On Aug. 3, 2002, after finishing nearly two years of construction, the company opened a store in Wichita, Kansas, at Towne East Square mall. A year later, the Wichita store hit its sales goals, despite entering the market during a time of record layoffs and a spiraling economy. In the March 11, 2003, issue of *Women's Wear Daily,* Jim commented on the road ahead for the company. "For the short-term, we're expanding in the Midwest, and from there we may take the chain national, depending on economic conditions," he said. "Our philosophy is steady, but well-planned growth. We open at least one or two new stores a year and usually only one or two stores per market. We take a micro-intensive approach to merchandising and buy based on a store's unique local needs. Our plan is always to build trust and loyalty by focusing on customer service, literally from the ground up."

In September 2003, Von Maur added locations in Louisville, Kentucky, at Oxmoor Center, and Ann Arbor, Michigan, at Briarwood Mall, followed by stores in Livonia, Michigan, at Laurel Park Place, and Glenview, Illinois, at The Glen Town Center. The Michigan and Kentucky stores were obtained at auction after Jacobsen Stores, Inc. filed for bankruptcy and liquidated its stores. "It was a whirlwind that year," Jim says. "But it was exciting to be part of it."

In 2003, Von Maur opens four new stores, including this one in Glenview, Illinois, at The Glen Town Center.

chapter 13

A WATERSHED YEAR IN RETAIL

In 2005, retail history would forever be changed when Federated Department Stores acquired the May Department Stores company for $11 billion. The deal created the nation's largest department store chain, with more than 1,000 stores and $30 billion in annual sales. It also caused the number of independent and regional department stores to dwindle even further as Marshall Field's, Hecht's, and Filene's disappeared under the Macy's name. While this mega-merger was in full bloom, Von Maur opened at Polaris Fashion Place in Columbus, Ohio—its first store in the Buckeye state.

On Oct. 23, 2005, a *Des Moines Register* article called Von Maur "an anomaly in the revolving door of department store chains. The family-owned business has been growing in the last five years, while many department stores are closing or being gobbled up by larger chains." One retail consultant told the *Register*, "Being a private company, Von Maur has been able to grow slowly and rationally. It takes advantage of opportunities that make sense for it and where it can differentiate itself in a market."

Over the next two years, the company would make further changes, launching online shopping in 2007 and closing its Westdale Mall store in Cedar Rapids, Iowa. In September 2008, Von Maur opened a store at The Greene lifestyle center in Beavercreek, a suburb of Dayton, Ohio. The store gave Dayton its first new, upscale department store in nearly a

Von Maur launches
online shopping in 2007.

Von Maur's online sales expanded quickly, prompting the company to create a specialized studio to photograph the newest apparel and accessories.

decade. Two months later, on Nov. 8, 2008, Von Maur opened at Corbin Park lifestyle center in Overland Park, Kansas. The mall opened as phase one of a 1.1 million-square-foot, open-air shopping village. Within six months, the U.S. economy would take one of its worst turns in history, marked by record unemployment and a spiraling stock market. Almost daily, companies announced they were closing stores, slowing expansion plans, or ceasing operations altogether. Macy's announced in January 2009 it was closing 11 stores. It was a tough time for all retailers, and some analysts worried the new Von Maur stores in Ohio and Kansas wouldn't survive. A reporter from the *Dayton Daily News* interviewed Von Maur representatives on March 14, 2009, six months after The Greene opened. "The retail industry had its worst holiday shopping season in decades and has retrenched during a severe recession in which department stores' same-store sales dropped 9 percent in February from a year earlier," the article states. "It's hardly the kind of environment that nurtures new stores. Yet a Von Maur spokeswoman said the privately held company hasn't changed course or wavered in its commitment to customer service."

Revenues were slightly off, but Von Maur had not reduced any of its staff. Jim says Von Maur benefited from not overreaching during the industry's boom years, maintaining a lean corporate structure, and seeing significant online sales increases by 2010. "The irony is that we weren't sure at first if the internet was the real deal," Jim says. "So we just put a few key items online to test them. Soon, we couldn't keep up with the orders and realized this was the future." It became clear Von Maur needed more space for its fledgling ecommerce business. "We had been operating it in a small corner of our corporate distribution center—in a space about the size of a small garage," Jim says with a chuckle. "We had no infrastructure in place to handle the orders coming in." Before long, Von Maur built a separate ecommerce facility, adjacent to its corporate headquarters, and invested in a sophisticated warehousing robotics system.

While online orders were gaining ground, Von Maur surprised the industry again in 2010 when it announced plans to move into new markets in the South, Northeast, and Southeast. Von Maur opened in Lake St. Louis, Missouri, at The Meadows on Sept. 18, 2010. Then, in rapid succession, the company opened three new stores in Georgia: one in metro Atlanta at North Point Mall in Alpharetta in 2011; one, almost exactly one year to the day later in 2012, at Perimeter Mall in Atlanta; and then in 2016, at the Mall of Georgia, which is the largest mall in Georgia and one of the largest in the United

States. The company's vision was to use the Atlanta stores as flagship locations to expand farther into the South. "We've seen exciting growth in the South," Jim told the *Atlanta Journal-Constitution.* "We want to be part of that. Never in our wildest dreams did we think we would open a store in Atlanta. It's a dream come true." Jim went on to say he hoped to open four or five stores in the Atlanta area. "We'd like to surround the whole city, if we could. We want to serve the whole community."

America's Research Group Chairman Britt Beemer was quoted in the *Atlanta Journal-Constitution* as saying metro Atlanta, which is home to nearly 6.1 million people, was a good test market for the company as it explored entering the South. Beemer says department store expansion is "almost an extinct possibility anymore" as the number of large stores shrinks. "Atlanta's a pretty juicy market now," he said. "It's a big deal, what they're doing. I'm sure it was not undertaken

frivolously." Melody Wright, Von Maur chief operating officer, agreed, telling the *Dayton Daily News.* "I would say less than 5 percent of retailers are talking about what next store to open, and we're one of them."

By 2013, on the heels of the Atlanta openings, the company broke new ground in the Northeast and Southwest and moved farther into the South. Von Maur took over a former Bon-Ton location in the suburbs of Rochester, New York, at Eastview Mall; opened at Riverchase Galleria in Birmingham, Alabama; and moved into Quail Springs Mall in Oklahoma City. The Oklahoma store is the first to include a storm shelter, which is partially underground and can hold up to 430 people. The walls are 10 inches thick and are built to withstand a direct hit by a tornado. The company also opened its first store in the Milwaukee market at The Corners of Brookfield on April 8, 2017.

Von Maur opened three stores in the Atlanta area over five years, including at the Mall of Georgia on Sept. 17, 2016.

In 2012, Von Maur announced it would substantially increase the size of its ecommerce fulfillment center in Davenport, Iowa, which featured a sophisticated warehousing robotics system. *Chain Store Age* reported that the expansion reflected the company's successful online business at vonmaur.com, which had seen a triple-digit percentage increase.

By 2015, Von Maur's distribution system had grown to include 84 of its own trailers as represented here by its custom die-cast replica.

chapter 14

A RETURN TO DRY GOODS

As Von Maur department stores were popping up in new markets and the online business was growing, the company simultaneously launched a new chain of specialty stores called Dry Goods. The small, mall-based stores cater to a junior contemporary customer. From 2010 to 2017, Von Maur opened 27 Dry Goods stores in eight states, including Iowa, Illinois, Indiana, Kentucky, Michigan, Minnesota, Ohio, and Wisconsin. "The new store name was inspired by the von Maurs' original downtown dry goods store that opened in 1872," says Lindsay Caltagirone, vice president of Dry Goods for Von Maur. "All of the design elements were influenced by the von Maurs' earliest store."

Dry Goods was built to offer a boutique feel, featuring an ornate storefront with a pair of glass double doors that invite shoppers into the space. The store was designed collaboratively and features black and white mosaic tile floor, tin ceiling, schoolhouse-style light fixtures, and vintage-style artifacts.

Dry Goods has become a trendy fashion destination for young women and has followed in the steps of its parent company, offering interest-free credit with the new slogan, "Be Interesting. Not Interest Bearing."

"We look forward to building upon the tremendous success we have experienced thus far by continuing to expand the Dry Goods brand across the country," Caltagirone says.

Starting in 2010, the company launched a new chain of specialty stores called Dry Goods. In seven years, more than 27 of the mall-based stores had opened in eight states.

Known for offering the latest in junior contemporary clothing and accessories, Dry Goods features products from leading brands and offers an interest-free credit card for its customers. The store's décor features the chain's vintage, turn-of-the-century aesthetic.

THE FUTURE OF VON MAUR & DRY GOODS

Jim von Maur's long-term vision is to open new Dry Goods and Von Maur stores from coast to coast.

"I think customers all over America would love to shop with us," Jim says. "We're proud of the old-fashioned business principles that have gotten us this far. And I think if we stick with them, yet change with the times when necessary, we'll remain one of the nation's last independent, family-owned-and-operated department stores for a long time to come."

"Our goal, as we continue to grow, is to preserve the unique, customer-focused experience my great-grandfather, C.J. von Maur, envisioned when he founded the company," Jim von Maur says. "I am incredibly proud of that tradition, and it's one that will continue no matter where our stores or the industry might take us in the coming decades."

1872

J.H.C. Petersen & Sons Co. is founded on West Second Street in Davenport, Iowa.

1916

Harned & Von Maur purchases J.H.C. Petersen & Sons Co. and continues to operate the stores separately.

1961

Petersen's expands to Moline, Illinois, and purchases a furniture store in Orchard Center Shopping Plaza. The store closes Feb. 15, 1982.

1972

Petersen's celebrates a century of operation and opens the company's first mall store in Bettendorf, Iowa, at Duck Creek Plaza in June. The store closes on Sept. 12, 1999.

1887

Boston Store is established on the southwest corner of Second and Brady in Davenport, Iowa. Owners are C.J. von Maur, R.H. Harned, and E.C. Pursel.

1928

Harned & Von Maur and J.H.C. Petersen & Sons Co. stores merge and become Petersen Harned Von Maur, which customers dubbed "Petersen's."

1968

Petersen's purchases Van Allen Department Store on February 1 in downtown Clinton, Iowa.

1889

Pursel dies and Boston Store becomes "Harned & Von Maur."

1929

The retailer purchases an existing department store in Moline, Illinois, called Fisk and Loosley. The von Maurs closed the store in 1932.

1970

Petersen's purchases M.L. Parker Co. department store, at Second and Brady in Davenport, Iowa. The store closes July 31, 1971.

1974

Petersen's opens a store in SouthPark Mall in Moline, Illinois, on February 27.

VON MAUR STORE LOCATIONS

Riverchase Galleria
Hoover, Alabama
11/2/13

North Point Mall
Alpharetta, Georgia
11/5/11

Perimeter Mall
Atlanta, Georgia
11/10/12

Mall of Georgia
Buford, Georgia
09/17/16

Charlestowne Mall
St. Charles, Illinois
10/1/01

Hickory Point Mall
Forsyth, Illinois
8/5/89

SouthPark Mall
Moline, Illinois
2/27/74

The Glen Town Center
Glenview, Illinois
10/18/03

The Shoppes at College Hills
Normal, Illinois
8/12/89

Yorktown Center
Lombard, Illinois
7/18/94

Castleton Square Mall
Indianapolis, Indiana
9/26/98

Greenwood Park Mall
Greenwood, Indiana
10/24/98

Jefferson Pointe
Fort Wayne, Indiana
8/6//01

College Square Mall
Cedar Falls, Iowa
3/1/87

Lindale Mall
Cedar Rapids, Iowa
10/7/81

NorthPark Mall
Davenport, Iowa
9/3/81

DRY GOODS LOCATIONS (as of 2017)

ILLINOIS

Fox Valley Mall, Aurora

Market Place, Champaign

Oakbrook Center, Oak Brook

Orland Park Mall, Orland Park

Woodfield Mall, Schaumburg

Hawthorn Center, Vernon Hills

Westfield Old Orchard, Skokie

INDIANA

Glenbrook Square Mall, Fort Wayne

Greenwood Park, Greenwood

Fashion Mall, Indianapolis

University Park Mall, Mishawaka

IOWA

Coral Ridge Mall, Coralville

Jordan Creek Mall, West Des Moines

KENTUCKY

Fayette Mall, Lexington

Mall St. Matthews, Louisville

1975

Petersen's expands to Iowa's state capital on August 4 with a store in Valley West Mall, West Des Moines, Iowa.

1979

Petersen's opens a store in Muscatine, Iowa, on August 24. The store closes on Dec. 24, 1994.

1980

The retailer opens at Westdale Mall on September 6 in Cedar Rapids, Iowa. The store closes on Jan. 31, 2007.

1981

Petersen's opens three Iowa stores. On September 3, the company opens NorthPark Mall in Davenport. Two stores open on October 7: Cedar Rapids' Lindale Mall and Iowa City's Sycamore Mall.

1986

Petersen's closes its flagship downtown Davenport store on October 1.

1987

Petersen's opens another Iowa store on March 1 at College Square Mall in Cedar Falls.

1989

The company purchases two Illinois stores: one at Hickory Point Mall near Decatur and the other at College Hills Mall in Normal. Both stores open in August.

1989

Jack Arth becomes the first person outside the von Maur family to be named president of the company.

Petersen Harned Von Maur shortens its name to Von Maur.

1990

Company headquarters relocates on February 19 from the former Petersen's downtown Davenport store to a location on the north side of Davenport near Interstate 80. Downtown offices close on March 1.

1994

Von Maur enters the Chicago market, opening a new flagship store in Lombard, Illinois, at Yorktown Center on July 18.

1995

Von Maur expands outside of the Iowa-Illinois area and into Omaha, Nebraska, on August 5 at Westroads Mall.

1998

Von Maur purchases two stores in the Indianapolis area at Castleton Square Mall and Greenwood Park Mall.

1999

The Lincoln, Nebraska, store at SouthPointe Pavilions opens on August 7.

2001

Von Maur opens three stores: Eden Prairie Center in Eden Prairie, Minnesota, on July 30; Jefferson Pointe in Fort Wayne, Indiana, on August 6; and Charlestowne Mall in St. Charles, Illinois, on October 1.

2002

Von Maur opens a store in Wichita, Kansas, at Towne East Square on August 3.

2003

Von Maur opens two new stores in Michigan: Ann Arbor at Briarwood Mall and Livonia at Laurel Park Place. The company also opens stores in Louisville, Kentucky, at Oxmoor Center and in Glenview, Illinois, at The Glen Town Center.

2005

Von Maur opens at Polaris Fashion Place in Columbus, Ohio, on Nov. 5, 2005.

2007

Von Maur launches online shopping.

2008

Von Maur opens at The Greene in Dayton, Ohio, on September 13, creating the city's first new traditional department store in nearly a decade. Von Maur also opens Corbin Park Lifestyle Center in Overland Park, Kansas, on November 8.

2010

Von Maur opens in Lake St. Louis, Missouri, at The Meadows on September 18. The company also introduces a new store concept called Dry Goods aimed at young women. The first Dry Goods store opens in Aurora, Illinois, in October.

The company also opens an ecommerce fulfillment center near its corporate headquarters.

2011

Von Maur opens in metro Atlanta's North Point Mall in Alpharetta, Georgia, on November 5.

2012

Von Maur opens a second store in metro Atlanta at Perimeter Mall in Dunwoody, Georgia, on November 10.

2013

Von Maur moves its Iowa City store to Coralville, Iowa, at Iowa River Landing and opens two stores in a week: one in the suburbs of Birmingham Alabama, and another outside Rochester, New York, marking the family's first foray into the Northeast.

2014

Von Maur opens a store just outside of Oklahoma City—the family's first store in the Southwest.

2016

Von Maur opens its third Atlanta-based store at the Mall of Georgia, the largest mall in Georgia and one of the largest in the United States.

2017

Von Maur moves into the Milwaukee market by opening at The Corners in Brookfield on April 8.

Right: Circa 1910, Petersen's department store on Second Street in downtown Davenport.

(Photo courtesy Putnam Museum of History and Natural Science)

Iowa River Landing
Coralville, Iowa
10/7/81

Valley West Mall
West Des Moines, Iowa
8/4/75

Corbin Park
Overland Park, Kansas
11/8/08

Towne East Square
Wichita, Kansas
8/3/02

Oxmoor Center
Louisville, Kentucky
9/20/03

Briarwood Mall
Ann Arbor, Michigan
9/20/03

Laurel Park Place
Livonia, Michigan
10/18/03

Eden Prairie Center
Eden Prairie, Minnesota
7/30/01

The Meadows
Lake St. Louis, Missouri
9/18/10

SouthPointe Pavilions
Lincoln, Nebraska
8/7/99

Westroads Mall
Omaha, Nebraska
8/5/95

Eastview Mall
Victor, New York
10/26/13

Quail Springs Mall
Oklahoma City, Oklahoma
10/18/14

Polaris Fashion Place
Columbus, Ohio
11/5/05

The Greene Towne Center
Beavercreek, Ohio
9/13/08

The Corners of Brookfield
Brookfield, Wisconsin
4/8/2017

MICHIGAN

Briarwood Mall, Ann Arbor

Woodland Mall, Kentwood

Twelve Oaks Mall, Novi

MINNESOTA

Southdale Center, Edina

Ridgedale Center, Minnetonka

Apache Center, Rochester

Rosedale Center, Roseville

Crossroads Center, St. Cloud

OHIO

Kenwood Towne Center, Cincinnati

WISCONSIN

Fox River Mall, Appleton

West Towne Mall, Madison

Mayfair Mall, Wauwatosa

A GLIMPSE AT SOME OF THE NATION'S FAMILY-OWNED DEPARTMENT STORES THAT HAVE CLOSED THEIR DOORS*

Abraham & Straus
Adler's
Addis & Dey
Alexander's
B. Altman
AM&A
Anderson-Newcombe
Arbaugh's
Auerbach's
L.S. Ayres
Bacon's
Bamberger's
Battelstein's
Bendel's
L.L. Berger
Bergner's
Bernheimer-Leader
Best & Co.
Blach's
James Black Co.
Gus Blass
Block's
Block & Kuhl
Boggs & Buhl
Bon-Marche [WA & NC]
Bonwit Teller
Boston Store
Boylan-Pierce
H. H. Bowman
Brach Thompson
Brandeis
Braunstein's
John Bressmer
Brett's
Brintnall's
The Broadway
Brock's
Brody's
John A. Brown
Brown's
Buffums
Bugbee's
Bullock's
Burdines
Burger Phillips
Bush & Bull
Cain-Sloan

Calendar, McAuslan & Troupe
The Carl Co.
Carlisle's
Castner-Knott
Chappell's
T.A. Chapman
City of Paris
Clark's
M.M. Cohn
Arnold Constable
Craig's
Crosby Bros.
Cox's
The Crescent
Crowley-Milner
Dalton's
Daniels & Fisher
Davison's
Dayton's
De Lendrecie
DeLoach
Denholm's
Denver Dry Goods
Desmond's
The Diamond
Donaldson's
Dunlap's
Dunnavant's
Eastman Bros. & Bancroft
Edgar's
E.W. Edwards & Son
Ellis, Stone & Co.
Emery, Bird, Thayer
Emporium-Capwell
Epstein's
Espenhain's
The Fair [multiple]
Famous-Barr
Filene's
Flah's
Foley's
Forbes & Wallace
Fowler, Dick & Walker
Fowler's
B. Forman
Fox
Frank & Seder

Franklin-Simon
Frederick & Nelson's
H. Freedlander Co.
Frost Bros.
Froug's
Furchgott's
Wm. F. Gable Co.
Gabriel's
Garfinckel's
Gayfer's
John Gerber Co.
Gertz
Gilchrist's
Gilmore Bros.
Gimbels
Gladdings
Glass Block
The Globe Store
Godchaux's
Golds
Goldblatt's
Goldenberg Co.
Goldsmith's
Goldstein-Migel
Goldwater's
Gottschalk's
Goudchaux's
W.T. Grant
Grieve
Grossman's
Gutman's
Bisset & Holland
Hahne's
Hale Bros.
Halle's
Halliburton's
Hamburger & Sons
L. Hammel
Harris
Harris-Emery
Harvey's
Harzfeld's
Hearn's
Hecht's
Heer's
S.H. Heironimus
Hemphill-Wells

Hengerer's
Hennessy's
Hens & Kelly
Henshey's
Herberger's
Herbst
Herpolsheimer's
Hink's—Hinkle's
Hinshaw's
Hochschild-Kohn
D.H. Holmes
Hudson's
Hutzler's
Innes
Iszard's
Ivey's
Jacobson's
Jacome's
Jellefs
Jenss
The Jones Store
Jones & Jones
Jordan-Marsh
Joseph Horne
Joske's
Joslin's
Kahn's
Kann's
Karroll's
Katz
Kaufman's
Kaufmann's
Kennington's
Kerr's
Kessler's
Killian's
Kilpatrick's
S. Klein
Kline's
J.W. Knapp
Korrick's
Krauss's
Lamont's
Lamson's
Lane's—Lansburgh's
LaSalle's
F&R Lazarus

Leggett	Montgomery Fair	J.W. Robinson's	Strouss-Hirshberg
H. Leh & Co.	Muller's	Rogers	Swanson's
Leonard's	Myer's Bros.	Ronzon's	Tapp's
Levy's	Namm's	Root's	John Taylor Dry Goods
J.R. Libby	Neusteter's	Rorabaugh-Buck	W. Taylor Co.
Liberty House	Newman's	Rose's	Thalhimer's
Lintz	O'Connor-Moffatt	Rosenbaum's	Tichte-Goettinger
Lion	Ohrbach's	Rosenwald's	Tiedtke's
Lipman's	M. O'Neil	Roshek's	Troutman's Emporium
Lit Brothers	O'Neill's	Rothschild & Sons	The Union
Frederick Loeser's	Orr's	Rubenstein's	Upton's
Loveman's	The Outlet	Russell's	Van Arsdale's
B. Lowenstein	The Palace	Sage-Allen	Vandever's
A.W. Lucas	Palais-Royal	Sakowitz	Walker's
Maas Brothers	The Paris	Sanger-Harris	Walker Bros.
Mabley & Carew	Parisian Stores	Scarborough's	Walker-Scott
I. Magnin	B. Peck	Scranton Dry Goods	John Wanamaker
Joseph Magnin	Peck's Dry Goods	Schreiner's	H.P. Wasson
Edward Malley	Peerless	Schuneman & Evans	Watt & Shand
Mandel Brothers	Pelletier's	Schuster's	Week's
Manchester's	Penn Traffic	Scruggs, Vandervoort, Barney	Weichmann's
J. Mandelbaum & Sons	People's Department Store	Selber Bros.	Weinstock's
Maison Blanche	Perkins-Timberlak	Shepard's	Chas. V. Weise
Marshall Field's	Pfieffer	Shillito's	J.B. White
Marston's	Pizitz	Shriver's	The White House
Martin's	H&S Pogue	Sibley's	[Calif. & Texas]
May Company	Polsky's	Siegel-Cooper	White & Kirk
May-Cohen	Pomeroy's	Thos. Smiley & Co.	R.H. White's
Mays	Popular Dry Goods	Smith & Welton	Whitner's
McAlpin's	Porteous, Mitchell & Braun	Smith & Wilkins	Wieboldt's
McClurklan's	Porter's	Snellenburg's	Wilkin's
McCreery's	Powers	Ben Snyder Co.	Wilmington Dry Goods
McCurdy's	H.C. Prange	Jos. A. Spiess	Woodward & Lothrop
G.M. McKelvey—McRae's	Proffitt's	Steiger's	Wolf & Dessauer
R.A. McWhirr	Walter Pye's	Steinbach	Woolf Bros.
Meier & Frank	Quackenbush	R. H. Stearn's	Wolff & Marx
Meis	Read's	Steinfeld's—Steinmart's	Edward Wren Co.
Meyers-Arnold	J. Redelsheimer	Stekete's	Wurzburg's
I. Miller	Regenstein's	Sterling-Lindner	Yetter's
Miller & Paine	Rhodes	Stern's	Young Quinlan
Miller's	Rices-Nachmans	Charles A. Stevens	ZCMI
Miller & Rhoads	Rich's	Stewart's [MD & TX]	Zollinger-Harned
Mills Dry Goods	Richard's	Stix, Baer, & Fuller	
Edward C. Minas	Rike's	Stone Thomas	
Missoula Mercantile Co.	Rines Bros.	Strawbridge & Clothier	
Monnig's	Robeson's	Stripling's	

* Source: Jan Whitaker, author of *Service and Style: How the American Department Store Fashioned the Middle Class.*
The von Maurs regret any omissions or errors.

AUTHOR'S NOTE AND BIBLIOGRAPHY

I would like to thank the many people who helped gather information, insights, and photos for this book, particularly Chuck, Dick, and Jim von Maur; Vivienne Holloway; Jack Arth; the Davenport Public Library; Butler University; and many Von Maur associates. The majority of the sources used in this book came from the Von Maur archives of store newsletters (*Petersen's Post What's in Store*) and items collected by the family and the company over the years.

Some external sources proved to be invaluable, including a book by Jan Whitaker, author of *Service and Style: How the American Department Store Fashioned the Middle Class*, which provided a broader context into how department stores grew, why they declined, and how they responded to and shaped the society around them. I also gleaned insights from *Not for Profit Alone, a Brief History of Petersen Harned Von Maur*, a 14-page summary of the company compiled by an unnamed source; and Paul Greenland's *Von Maur, Inc., International Directory of Company Histories*, Volume 64 (1993).

Melinda Pradarelli

OTHER SOURCES

1. The Davenport Public Library archives.

2. "A Corner for the People," poem and cartoon about the young Rowland Harned as appeared in "A Portfolio of Cartoons," published by the *Davenport Times,* 1912-1913. Verses by Irving C. Norwood.

3. Photo courtesy of the *Father of the Davenport Levee* by Hugh Harrison.

4. "The combined store carries stock in excess of $1 million," *Davenport Democrat and Leader,* May 7, 1928.

5. Fifth Avenue Fashions Ad, *The Daily Times,* Feb. 26, 1932.

6. Photo courtesy of *Moline: City of Mills,* 1998, Arcadia Publishing.

7. Photo courtesy of *The Daily Times,* May 2, 1942.

8. Kansas City Library Archives, Decade 50.

9. Petersen's 70th Anniversary Ad, 1942.

10. "Rugs and Plugs," *Time Magazine,* June 10, 1970.

11. "Celebrating their Sagas of Success," *Times Democrat,* April 30, 1972.

12. "Brandeis brings considerable clout to Des Moines," *Des Moines Register,* July 27, 1975.

13. "Building on Tradition…," *Quad City Times,* March 15, 1981.

14. "Saturday: A Guide to Eating Out. Homey Touch for Cafeteria," by Jim Arpy, Davenport library archives, date unknown.

15. "They keep on falling: And now, even Gibraltar," by Bill Wundrum, *Quad City Times.*

16. "The best thing we can do is treat a customer well, and they'll tell their friends," *Lombard Daily Herald,* 1994.

17. *Crain's Chicago Business.*

18. *Footwear News,* 1995.

19. *Women's Wear Daily,* Aug. 16, 1994, and March 11, 2003.

20. *Atlanta Journal-Constitution.*

21. *Dayton Daily News.*

22. *Moline: City of Mills* by David R. Collins, Rich J. Johnson, Bess Pierce, Arcadia Publishing, 1998.

23. "Once upon a time…," *Greater Baton Rouge Business Report,* Sept. 25, 2007.

24. Remembering the Great American Department Stores, www.DepartmentStoreHistory.net.

25. Emily Starbuck Gerson, www.creditcards.com/credit-card/credit-collectible-coins-charga-plate.

26. fundinguniverse.com/company-histories/Von-Maur-Inc-Company-History.

27. "A time of change: Company makes huge leaps with expansion, public-stock offering," by Kathy Mulady, *Seattle Post Intelligencer,* June 26, 2001.

28. *Iowan* Magazine, 1987.

29. Mississippi Ferry Boat photo credit www.qconline.com.

30. Mechanical Santa, photo credit, Nick Loomis, *Bettendorf News.*

31. *New York Times,* Nov. 21, 1988.

32. "The Media Business: After Years of Swimming, Newspapers Tread Water," by Albert Scardino, Nov. 21, 1988, http://query.nytimes.com/gst/fullpage.html?res=940D-E5D7113CF932A15752C1A96E948260&sec=&-spon=&pagewanted=all

33. "Yorktown Store Hopes Top Service Speaks for Itself," *Yorktown Daily Herald,* 1994.

34. 1999 Quad Cities artist John Holladay's colorful map that captured the company's growth.

35. "We had very frank and open discussions," *Quad Cities Times,* July 28, 1999.

36. "Von Maur: First-year sales strong," by Sherry Graham, *Wichita Business Journal,* Aug. 8, 2003.

37. *Crain's Chicago Business,* by Sandra Jones, Sept. 5, 2005.

38. *Dayton Business Journal,* Aug. 21, 2006.

39. Associate Press Images (AP Photo/Eric Francis), 12/7/2007.

INDEX

173